PRAISE FOR REVOLT WOMEN...

I'd love to live in a world where this book wasn't necessary – where women are no longer damned if they do and doomed if they don't. This deeply researched, profoundly thoughtful book may make you angry, but more importantly, it will inspire you to explore that 'sparkle of female genius' that allows women to take on the world in their later years. Bravo Lucy for shining a spotlight on the growing numbers of *Revolting Women*!

Emma Howard Boyd CBE, Former Chair of the Environment Agency, Chair of the Green Finance Institute

Our research at Cranfield University focuses on the lack of women in leadership in FTSE companies. Why are there so few women in those top executive roles? Dr Ryan supplies a compelling answer in sharing the experiences of senior women in business and the challenges they have in navigating menopause. Women don't lose their energy or their ambition midlife, but they do need support from their companies. Arguably the kinds of changes these women would like to make to the ways they work might benefit everyone and help to foster a truly inclusive workplace!

Professor Sue Vinnicombe CBE, Professor of Women & Leadership, co-author The Annual Female FTSE Board Report, Cranfield School of Management

This supremely well-researched and passionate book lifts the lid on the reality behind the story that 'we've done it!' in retaining our midlife professional women. Yes, we're talking and doing a lot about gender parity, but there is still so much work for businesses and society to engage with – and this book should be your companion. It gave me lightbulb moments throughout, sometimes shocking, but mostly inspiring. I felt hopeful at the extent that women want to work and contribute after midlife, despite the considerable 'blind eye' being turned to their exit. A relevant, timely book that should be pressed into the hands of every executive, male and female alike.

Claire Hughes, Commercial Director, The PHS Group

I love this book! It has questioned my beliefs as a business leader and as a woman. It has helped me better understand professional women at midlife and know I'm not the only one juggling the care of parents and children. And it has given me a lot of energy and excitement for the next phase of my career. So much to give back and, of course, so much to achieve!

Cristina Nestares, CEO, UK Insurance,
Admiral Group plc

This book is simply incredible - timely, relevant, ground-breaking, and profoundly honest. Grounded in lived experience of organizational realities, it tells stories, instead of waving slogans of diversity. Yet, informed by research, it looks beyond stories to systematically analyse and understand a widespread phenomenon, suggesting practical and positive ways forward.

Professor Ilona Boniwell, CEO Positran, Professor of Positive
Psychology at University of East London

I am proud to be one of Lucy Ryan's 'Revolting Women', having left corporate life and reinvented my career in my fifties. This is a rich, well-sourced, immensely thought-provoking book. Ryan is absolutely spot-on in calling for systemic change and urging the rest of us to be change advocates, to revolt against often unspoken assumptions that the 'youthful, male, full-time-led organization' is where it's still at. For every midlife woman who knows they have plenty of expertise and energy to give – and wonders why managers don't see that – read this and take heart. You are not alone, and you can thrive as a 'free-range' woman.

Philippa Thomas, Professional career coach, former
International & National BBC TV News Presenter

How fabulous to have Lucy Ryan in your corner! This is such a great call to arms – to business leaders, to the wider workforce, to women themselves – to recognize the 'grey capital' of menopausal women and harness their power in order to unleash its full potential. Particularly refreshing in Dr Ryan's account is the recognition of complexity in the arena of diversity. Bland assumptions are dispensed with tartly and in their place there is a scientific rigor which encourages compassion and flexibility in order to build truly innovative and competitive businesses with the help of some amazing women.

Catherine Des Forges, CEO, The Independent Cinema Organisation

Real life, factual and gripping – an honest account which unmasks the experiences of midlife women, makes the invisible visible and challenges the exasperating norm of our times. History will look back at the stories in this book and shake its head in disbelief. Why on earth was the conversation so hard? Written for revolting women (know you are more than enough, you are vital and you are not alone – you are part of an uprising that is not being so silent) and for those men who have the courage and insight to lead a revolt - you'll be taken beyond 'it's the right thing to do' (of course, it is) and find yourself with a sharp nudge in the ribs.

Have you heard it all before? Is this an optional read? The answer is a resounding 'No'. You need it and your business demands it.

Becky Hewitt, former Human Resources Director, Leeds Building Society

A thought-provoking and powerful book, which challenges readers to confront the reasons as to why women at the top of their game leave the workforce. This book has made me reflect on the kind of life and career I wish to have in my next decade. It has also made me confront some hard truths about what more I must do to create a workplace that aims to retain women at this life-stage.

Julie Ann Haines, CEO, Principality Building Society

This story needs to be told – so employees are heard and empowered, whilst employers understand and act. I hope this book can be a force for good in our society.

Ben Cooper, Chief Content and Music Officer,
Bauer Media Group

Revolting Women is a must-read guide for all HR professionals and managers who employ talented women in midlife. This engaging and insightful book by Lucy Ryan showcases the stories of intelligent, committed, and highly motivated women workers who are undervalued – and who choose to exit the workplace as a result. The book is fast-paced, incisive, and compelling – it gets right to the heart of why highly trained, capable women are leaving corporate lives to forge their own pathways in business. *Revolting Women* is an essential read for leaders seeking to prevent the exodus of talented midlife women from their workforce.

Professor Caroline Gatrell FAcSS, FBAM, Associate Dean
Research, University of Liverpool Management School

At last, the voices of midlife women have a powerful collective voice, thanks to Lucy Ryan. There are two big reasons senior leaders (not just HR) should not just read this (very readable) book, but act on it. First taking action to address why women are 'revolting' is the right thing to do. Second, the business case for doing the 'right thing'! In a world where talent is both scarce, especially experienced talent, and more and more expensive to hire, why not make more of what you have, and not enforce, bluntly out of date practices upon this wonderful, pool of (all too often overlooked) talent who will continue to bring their richness of lived experience and the diversity of thought that comes with it; and excitingly real evidence of inclusive leadership.

Simon Reichwald, Chief Progression Officer, Connectr

I devoured the excellent research and was really moved by the personal stories and experiences shared in this richly rewarding read. Lucy Ryan is a real talent – warm, pragmatic, and bold in her thinking. This thought-provoking book has given me a dose of confidence! It's a brilliant combination of insight and challenge, but she has also created a sense of community – we're not alone in this journey. I would love to have had the courage and skill to write this book. Imagine leaving your reader feeling privileged, uplifted, and energized. What a thing! Thank you, Lucy.

Janie van Hool, Director, *Voice Presence,* **Author,** *The Listening Shift* **(Business Book of the Year, 2022)**

Revolting Women is a courageous book, lifting the lid on the utter waste of talented women leaving the workplace. The book is well-evidenced, accessible, and research-based. A compelling read that combines laugh-out-loud moments with moments when I wanted to scream, recognizing the truth and reality in it for all those women who don't feel seen or heard in their organization. It is a hopeful book highlighting that whilst middle age can be a challenging time, it doesn't have to be the end of a rich and vibrant life, but rather the beginning of an adventure to discover our identity in the second half of life. Furthermore, it acts as a rallying cry for Chief People Officers to recognise what's going on with this demographic and take steps to avoid them voting with their hearts, minds, and ultimately, their feet!

Diane Herbert, Non-executive Director, NHS, former Human Resource Director, Channel 4

There is a different conversation to be had in this book: the sense-making of mid-life and the chance to define what you DON'T want to be! Lucy doesn't try to put menopausal women in one (hot and sweaty) box. She acknowledges and understands the difficulty that some women face, but she also helps to explore other side of it too: the positive experiences that are in direct contrast to the typical narrative. The book is pulled together with a really practical conclusion – loads of great questions to challenge ourselves and the organizations we work for with. I've already made a list of all of the people (not just women), I'm going to buy this book for!

Elaine Warwicker, Managing Director, Canny Conversations, Director, Women in Business Gloucestershire

Lucy is my inspirational coach. Through this book she brings forward some really uncomfortable insights that will stir your emotions and build your curiosity. Drawing on solid research and wonderful stories from real women *'Revolting Women'* is a rich source of insight and storytelling. Finally, the thinking on 'post traumatic growth' and the positivity this can lead to creates a powerful message of hope and direction.

Jill Johnston, Chief People Officer,
Cumberland Building Society

Always engaging, occasionally uncomfortable, this book should be read by every member of every board in the country. By dissecting why senior women are leaving organizations and offering practical solutions, maybe there is hope for the next generation of hugely talented female leaders.

Jacqui Brabazon, Trustee HACRO, Former Chief Marketing
Officer, JP Morgan International Private Bank

This is an important read for leaders and a hopeful one for women. Lucy Ryan cuts through the excuses and debunks myths as to why we are losing talented midlife women from the workforce. She uses research and stories and presents practical solutions for retaining critical female talent that allows midlife women to fulfil their potential. There's a call to arms for women and men to use their voice to make change happen and it needs to be heard from an economic, societal, and moral perspective.

Joelle Warren, Founding Partner, Warren Partners

A fresh look at the invisible forces of gendered ageism in the workplace – an optimistic and practical must read of how to get the most from the female workforce especially as they mature and offer more powerful experience to organizations and society. Women would not need to revolt or leave the workforce if Dr Ryan's words were heeded. A must read for everyone wanting to honour the rich experience of the female journey in the workplace.

Fiona Parashar, Founder and CEO,
Leadership Coaching Limited

REVOLTING WOMEN

WHY MIDLIFE WOMEN ARE WALKING OUT, AND WHAT TO DO ABOUT IT

LUCY RYAN

First published in Great Britain by Practical Inspiration Publishing, 2023

ISBN   9781788603980 (print)
        9781788604000 (epub)
        9781788603997 (mobi)

Want to bulk-buy copies of this book for your team and colleagues? We can customize the content and co-brand *Revolting Women* to suit your business's needs.

Please email info@practicalinspiration.com for more details.

Practical Inspiration Publishing

MIX
Paper | Supporting responsible forestry
FSC
www.fsc.org   FSC® C013604

TABLE OF CONTENTS

FOREWORD

This book will outrage you but hang on in there; it has a happy ending.

The fury comes from Lucy Ryan's crisp walk through the reality of a woman's working life. We struggle to get good jobs, wrestle with the conflicting demands of work and childcare and our careers are often held back by sexist bosses. Then, after we have developed our knowledge and skills over decades, comes the triple whammy of the menopause, caring for ageing parents, and helping teenagers through the UK's ghastly exam system. We learn to cope with those new trials but there's a career-killing blow to come. Those sexist bosses say we are now too old to be promoted and we are either forced out or we leave in disgust.

But Lucy shows that women are increasingly refusing just to crawl away from their careers. She talked in-depth to forty older women executives for this important piece of research. The majority were determined, not just to stay in their jobs, but to move up. Again and again, women told her that age had brought them new confidence and they felt they were just coming into their own. As Lucy puts it, the career clock ticks differently for women. Of her interviewees, 70% said they were ready to step up in their careers within or without their current organization. A fascinating fact she uncovers is that there has been a 67% increase in women over 55 opening new business accounts.

A key development has been the change in attitudes towards negative menopause symptoms which, according to official figures, drive a tenth of older women to give up work. Increasingly, women are demanding HRT to help. Good employers are starting to realise that it's bad business to train up a woman only to let her walk out of the door when she is at the peak of her abilities. Let's hope that the UK government, deeply worried by the loss of hundreds of thousands of workers since the pandemic, starts to realise that a major answer is to crack down on the outrage of employers' prejudice against older women.

I started a great new job at the age of 69. Queen Elizabeth II worked until she was 96. Fifty is young! Lucy demonstrates many older women have the energy and ambition to keep building their careers. We are the nation's untapped resource, and we have the right to work.

Every woman, every good employer, every politician, and every sexist boss should read this book.

Dorothy Byrne, President Murray Edwards College, University of Cambridge. Former Head of News & Current Affairs, Channel 4 Television

INTRODUCTION

Nothing in life is to be feared, it is only to be understood. Now is the time to understand more, so that we may fear less.

(Marie Curie, 1866–1934)

Just at the age women are in the position to progress in a significant way and assert their power in an organization, they step down, or worse, quit.[1] This is an extraordinary move. Here are women who have spent a professional lifetime facing into the everyday hurdles that working women will recognize: beating sexism by just getting through the door; overcoming societal expectations by demanding a pay rise; having kids and finding that 'having it all' is an indecent myth; working out how to co-parent; finding their voice, getting heard and starting to see the future they want.

And rather than being hailed by collective outrage (I'll even accept 'mild interest') their departure is greeted with silence. Silence from organizations, who turn a convenient blind eye to the unobtrusive drift of middle-aged women leaving their business; silence from the academic community who have but a handful of scholars interested in exploring the 'what's going on here?' And silence from women themselves, who – often surprised by the messiness of midlife – quietly exit the organization, gather their resources, and plan the next fulfilling chapter of their lives.

And this is the female midlife revolt. Less shouty and bloody than the French cry of *'vive la revolution!'* but no less powerful. A revolt against the expectations of the full on, no flex, head down senior management norm. A revolt against the discrimination that just gets louder for women the older they get, and a revolt against a patriarchal system that is changing at a glacial pace. *Why wait?* shout the women, as they throw their wisdom, experience, and energy into new projects, turning heads with their audacious new ventures. Revolting women!

The silent road to revolution

You might inherently recognize this revolt, but you're unlikely to have read much about it. And that's because two explanations dominate the answer as to *why do women quit at the top of their game?* Let's call these storylines 'Decline' and 'Freedom!' (always written with an exclamation mark).

The 'decline' narrative is the more robust, with our ageing bodies and minds apparently sagging, drooping, weakening, decaying, and generally dropping off the radar – literally and metaphorically – for the next 30 or so years.[2] The madness of menopause is mixed with our empty nest syndrome, and our foggy brains blended with our messed-up lives. It's a story that has been echoed through history, reiterated by women, retold in the media, and repeated at every possible turn.

The alternative 'Freedom!' narrative only got airspace a decade ago, showing middle-aged women absconding from their lives, heading into the sunset, free from all responsibilities, laughing all the way to the bank and the travel agency.[3] Women who have ditched their kids, partners, parents, and careers in aid of the 'good life'. Bolting, escaping, early retiring.

Both storylines give us an answer why women are leaving organizations, and both are fair answers, just not the whole picture. But both narratives do serve to maintain business as normal, with the responsibility for this picture placed fairly and squarely on the woman's shoulders. The middle-aged woman is either too mad, bad, or sad to take on a serious leadership role, with her responsibilities and physical problems proving unassailable, or she's not available. This is the 'woman problem'. That is, women can only blame themselves for their lack of success in the promotional field, their lack of self-confidence or their inability to juggle. Women are not confident enough; ambitious enough or resilient enough. They must 'lean in' and attend more workshops. They don't sell themselves well enough. Their bodies let them down. They are not young enough, pretty enough, or thin enough.

And if this seems far-fetched, you don't have to look further than the UK government-sponsored Hampton-Alexander review.[4] Both the Davies Report and Hampton-Alexander Reviews were annual reporting structures to check on the progress of women onto executive boards within FTSE 100 and FTSE 250/350 companies in the UK. In the absence of quotas, they have proved to be remarkable reporting bodies, holding companies to account for their board-level gender balance. In recent years, in the light of significant progress for non-executive female directors on boards yet glacial gains for full-time female executives, male executives were interviewed to understand their point of view. Three of the top ten answers given (see Chapter 2 for all ten) were that these midlife women were *not up for it; not able to do it; not available.*[5]

And so offered here in this book is a third storyline. A messier story for sure, because the midlife women I know and work with lead messy, intriguing, individual lives. But they are vibrant and energetic, discussing new and exciting phases of their professional lives, *despite* significant challenges, be they health, caring, relationship or financial matters.

This is a much less convenient storyline for those in power, though, as it requires organizations to engage with a systemic problem of gendered ageism,[6] and it is a story that necessitates facing into sustained discrimination, fixed mindsets and a system that favours the young.

A journey to revolt

Meet Eve.

Eve is 54. She is a mental health lead in the public sector who has worked her way up over 30 years and is in pole position for a senior leadership role. Eve describes herself as fit and robust, she is five years into the menopause, and on HRT to conquer her sleepless nights. She feels more attentive to, and in control of, her body. Eve feels liberated by her age, by the cessation of periods, and, as part of this liberation, has recently made the decision to go grey.

Eve has recently been given the feedback that she is not in the running for a director role, and has been advised to stay in her current job. The main reason given is that all director roles have been designed as full-time roles and Eve works a four-day week. With three teenage children, one daughter just 14 years old, that is as much as Eve believes she can work and still maintain a home presence. But Eve can also see she is being sidelined in a department surrounded by an executive team that is 80% male. Rather than being given her usual 'cut and thrust stuff', she describes being given 'great aunt responsibilities' – sitting, watching, overseeing, mentoring. She describes the toxic culture as bullish or bullying, with the leader describing the team in an interview as a 'kinda down the pub, sort it out, all mates, sorter-outers'. Ousted from closing a major financial deal Eve had led to that point, she was told she just 'wouldn't understand it'. Eve says it's well known across the organization that to challenge the culture is to limit your career, and she's aware she's backed off major problems, and chosen not to take out grievances, to protect her career. Rightly or wrongly, as she says.

But rather than remain stagnant in her career, Eve has decided to leave. On resigning, the (female) HR director responded, 'You lucky devil. I have a countdown clock on my computer telling me how many days, hours, I have to still work here.'

Eve was the first of my interviewees and my starting point for a five-year doctoral journey. I wanted to know how professional women experienced their midlife. I wanted to understand why they were leaving their jobs, where they were going and why. I needed to hear what was stopping this incredible talent from stepping up. I'm looking at my notes today as I write this chapter and see a list of questions that were buzzing around my head. Do people really believe older men are better leaders than older women? Have women given up the fight by this age? Are they happy to step out? Do organizations favour the young, the male, the full-time career path? Do women allow themselves to be overlooked? What happens when women lose patience with the system, seeking meaning at midlife beyond the company? Who's responsible for this problem?

Many thousands of hours were spent deep in rabbit holes of research, hundreds of hours of recorded interviews, accompanied by 40 courageous professional women, who bared their midlife souls to answer some fundamental questions about their lives, such as:

- What is your experience of middle age?
- What is it like to inhabit a middle-aged body?
- What's liberating/challenging about being older at this stage in your career?
- What assumptions do others have about your age?

- What influence does your current midlife have on your future career decisions?

From the start, I was naïve about the whole process of doing a PhD. An early exploration of the academic and management literature showed little research about professional middle-aged women, and there's something thrilling (and worrying!) about an area where you know your work will be unique. To do a PhD, you need a supervisor, and to get a supervisor you pitch your proposal to universities. I hadn't counted on the response from multiple universities to my research proposal, which, in a nutshell, went something like this:

University: Why do you want to study middle-aged, professional women?

Me: They're the largest demographic in our workforce, and I'm one.

University: There's very little literature about them.

Me: A gap in the literature! Sounds like a great idea to study them.

University: Will you be mentioning the menopause?

Me: Well since that is one of the major life experiences this group will go through, yes, it'll come up.

University: There really isn't enough of an audience for this kind of study.

Me: Because only half the population is affected by it?

It seemed that the largest workforce demographic was as invisible in academia as it seemed to be in business. From every university the response was the same – the proposal was 'unpublishable' or 'uninteresting'. It took one client, the indomitable Dorothy Byrne, then Editor at Large of Channel 4, now President of Murray Edwards College, Cambridge, to 'kick ass', knock down doors on my behalf and find a supervisor up for the challenge!

My findings in a nutshell

My doctoral findings would show that women at midlife are quitting the workplace for three reasons:

1. The maintenance of power
2. The collision of midlife changes
3. A revolution against gendered ageism

The maintenance of power

Whilst middle-aged women are the largest workforce demographic, once they reach positions of power, midlife women are commonly, and systemically, excluded from organizations on three counts. They are not male; they are not young; and they rarely follow linear careers. Perhaps more shocking is how this exclusion is normalized. That is, exclusionary language and practices are so deeply embedded within the organizational setting they are invisible and ignored.

The collision of midlife changes

Not only this, but my data showed the manifold changes at midlife can project women into a transition period as they cope with biological, social, and psychological transformation. Midlife can present women with a unique collision of 'stuff', from menopause to older motherhood, parental care, familial health issues and grief. It's a whirlwind that can scoop you up, leaving you breathless.

A revolution against gendered ageism

But. And this is a big *but*. In emerging from this hiatus, the voices of the women in my study spoke loudly of a desire for progress and achievement; of a need to step up in their organization and be celebrated for their knowledge and experience. Indeed, a significant finding was that 70% *of the women wanted to step up in their careers.* Not opt out, step down, move sideways, but up. These are women who firmly reject the notion of 'decline', or 'escape to retirement', and who are seeking flexible ways to navigate the significant issues surrounding their lives at this age, whilst still actively pursuing career advancement.

This is the third storyline – these are our revolting women and if they can't step up within your company, they'll do it on their own. That is, their lives have changed, their needs have changed, and if this cannot be considered, they will leave. As will their expertise. According to the Office for National Statistics, these 'oldpreneurs' (a dubious name) make up a fifth of Britain's new business owners, with a 67% increase in women over 55 opening business accounts in the last decade.[7] Data from the Federation of Small Business demonstrates women-led businesses contribute a staggering £105 billion GVA (gross value added) to the UK economy.[8] But this productive profitability represents a loss for their former employers!

Back to Eve.

Two years after our first interview, I returned to talk with Eve. I was curious to know what happened after her resignation. She described her sense of loss on leaving her organization, a grief after 30 years of employment. But within a year, Eve had set up her own counselling business, currently with a waiting list for patients. Within two years, Eve had added to her existing psychological and therapeutic training with yoga and mindfulness qualifications and is currently leading a series of world-first mindfulness retreats for medical practitioners in a post-Covid world. Eve has never been happier, in more demand, or more fulfilled. Her gain is her employers' loss.

Why do you need this book?

This book is about understanding and preventing the exodus of talented midlife women from your workforce and is relevant to you on three counts:

1. Your ageing talent is draining away
2. It makes business sense
3. It's the right/legal thing to do

It comes as no surprise to you that the workforce is ageing. As the proportion of the working population between 50 and state pension age will increase to 34% by 2050 in the UK,[9] many organizations are recognizing that their productivity and economic success will be increasingly tied to the success of their ageing workforce. This is particularly critical when it's linked with the shortage of skilled workers, with the Learning and Work Institute estimating a shortfall of 2.5 million highly skilled workers by 2030.[10] This talent drain is prevalent across the workforce, leaking wisdom and energy out of the corporation, which is acute for women over 50. These are the people who experience a collision of physical, emotional, and practical challenges at midlife – juggling menopause and older motherhood, together with the care for, and loss of, parents. And this has only been exacerbated by the fallout from Covid-19.[11] But as my data stresses, these are talented and powerful women. Invisible women who want to stay but are either overlooked or not being reached out to.

And the business case for the retention of professional women is made time and again in reports from management consultancies such as McKinsey Consulting, Bain & Co. and Cranfield University, with abundant statistics highlighting the increased performance of a company with diverse management and leadership teams.[12] Just one example emphasized that companies with a top quartile representation of women in executive committees (average age 45–55 years) perform significantly better (+47% return on equity and +55% average return on earnings) than companies with limited or no female representation.[13]

Equality, diversity, and inclusion (EDI) remain high in the concerns on the HR professional's agenda. This is evidenced in the CIPD's 2020 report on the top priorities for HR up to 2030, with two of the five concerns centred on diversity.[14] Not only do companies have a legal obligation to take their D&I agenda seriously, but your employees are also demanding to see this on your agenda. And so, not before time, diversity, inclusion, and belonging are increasingly becoming a moral agenda, with HR leading with a principle- rather than a policy-led approach.

The right side of revolting

Or perhaps you're a revolting woman – or know one? Please join my ranks! Not in decline, or over the hill. Not retiring but right on the cusp of the next chapter of your life. Reaching midlife, bored with the predictable stories you hear about your future, railing against the assumptions about your age and seeking a reframe for what success could look like. Or perhaps you'd like to read about women just like you and feel less alone? And if you're younger, let this book be a 'call to arms' for you, a way to navigate what lies ahead and, more importantly, to drive change before another generation of women is marginalized. My hope is to pose questions and suggest answers. To replace the black and white narrative with one of difference, of nuance. One of compassion and of motivation. A shift of language.

Within these pages

This book blends history with science, practical strategies with real voices. Each of the three parts of this book examines the evidence as to why women at midlife leave their organizations. Part 1 examines the issues of power. How is power maintained and how is the opposition weakened? What is it like for women to age in the workplace (and is it any different for men)? Together we'll explore the dominant myths and assumptions from a societal, corporate, and historical point of view. Part 2 takes a deep dive into the critical collisions of midlife for women. Think menopause, caring issues, and the bigger existential questions about the next chapter of life. Part 3 explains why women revolt and the nature of their brilliant resilience – or, as I highlight, the sparkle of female genius! Part 3 is full of optimism and hope. Where have women risen above the prejudice to succeed, and what are organizations doing to facilitate their success? The conclusion offers a positive agenda for change. With ten provocations, abundant questions, and exercises, I dare you to actually do something!

Throughout these pages you'll hear the voices of the women I interviewed. Whilst they are anonymized, you will recognize their stories. You will recognize the voices of professional women who have faced a lifetime of discrimination and scrambled through their professional midlives. Women who have 'made it' and are experiencing success, or the voices of those who have silently left your business. Or maybe you are one of these women? Women who have unspent creativity, an appetite for life, wondering where they now fit into society. Women with messy, unpredictable, menopausal bodies. Extraordinary, resilient, wise, funny, and brilliant women. This book is for revolting women: women just like you?

PART 1

POWER

There must be more equality established in society, or morality will never gain ground, and this virtuous equality will not rest firmly even when founded on a rock, if one half of mankind be chained to its bottom by fate, for they will be continually undermining it through ignorance or pride.

(Mary Wollstonecraft,
A Vindication of the Rights of Woman, 1792)

CHAPTER 1

PROBLEM, WHAT PROBLEM?

For most of history, Anonymous was a woman.
(Virginia Woolf, *Orlando*, 1928)

Middle-aged women are now powerful. In fact they run the show. We see them on our screens, on our radios, and heading up our organizations and political bodies. Just in the last decade, we're seeing older female sports presenters; we're listening to podcasts on midlife; hearing middle-aged female DJs; reading books authored by women past 50 years; and watching TEDx presentations by inspirational female business leaders. At least this is what the media would like us to believe. 'They're everywhere!' screamed a recent media report.[1]

It appears that many business leaders agree.[2] Bain & Co., management consultants who publish influential gender parity reports in the US and UK, led with this startling upfront statement,

> *Many male leaders believe the playing field is now level and that gender parity no longer needs to be a corporate priority. The data doesn't agree with this view.*

> *And neither do women.*

And there's research that agrees with these male leaders.[3] In a study by feminist scholars Adelina Broadbridge and Ruth Simpson, looking back at 25 years of gender and management studies, women are being presented as having a clear advantage in the leadership race, with their supposed preference for collaborative working and emotional awareness. The authors suggest that this poses a challenge for anyone undertaking gender research, 'It's being positioned as "old fashioned" and "redundant" in a world where, despite evidence to the contrary, gender issues are perceived to be solved.'

The missing 919 women

However, take any sector, any organization, public or private, and senior female professionals will still be in the minority, and according to the global non-profit organization Catalyst, this is commonly by a ratio of some 10:1.[4] For example, according to the Fawcett Society's Sex and Power 2022 index,[5] which provides a breakdown of percentages of women in power across UK politics, business, and public life, less than 2 in 5 posts in schools management go to women (up by just 1 percentage point in two years); 17% of social media CEOs and 22% of museum and gallery chairs are female; and 15% of sport governing bodies are led by a woman. Women across the pond fare no better with 14% of US financial institutions headed up by a woman[6] and 12% female leaders in the global energy sector.[7] Or my favourite statistic, known in the US as the 'John problem' – there are more CEOs named John leading Fortune 500 companies, than there are women in this role (or Peter, apparently, in the UK).[8] And just as a sidenote to enrage you, according to a study by Art UK, of almost 1,500 statues in London, those that feature animals are double those of named women![9]

And as for women of colour, in the UK they are simply missing altogether from the highest levels in many sectors.[10] In top roles, such as Supreme Court Justices, Metro Mayors, Police and Crime Commissioners, departmental Permanent Secretaries, FTSE 100 chief executives and General Secretaries of the largest trade unions, there are no women of colour represented. As for other intersecting characteristics such as disability, LGBTQ+ identity, class or religion, the data is, simply, missing.[11] Just not collected, let alone published. In the UK only eight women, and no women of colour, are currently employed as CEOs in the FTSE 100, while women only hold 14% of executive directorships and 38% of all directorships.[12] The Fawcett Society's Sex and Power 2022 report states, 'overall, across 5,166 positions of power in society, we found that women make up just under a third – 32% – of the total. That means 919 women are missing from the top roles.'[13]

And what does this have to do with age? Well, everything. Indeed, it's the sole factor that is common to all senior positions across the world. Research from the World at Work, 2022,[14] shows that the average age of someone in a senior position is around 56 years. Slightly higher if you're a board member (averaging 62 years for men and 59 years for women), and around 45 years for a senior manager. According to the Diligent Institute, who studied 5,000 public companies across the western world, the age bracket with the highest representation for directors is the 50–65 age bracket.[15]

A journey of 136 years

Essentially there is a weary familiarity with gender statistics, and little has changed since I read a business article a decade ago, 'Top 100 CEOs in the world', and stared at a sea of male faces. Fast forward to today and the statistics are, well, not a whole lot better. Let's take a swift romp across the world:

- Women currently hold 6.4% of CEO positions at S&P 500 companies and 5% in FTSE 350 companies (Catalyst, 2022)[16]

- In the Asia Pacific, 32% of heads of business are women, with just 10% of women holding management roles in India, 4% in Pakistan and 15% in Japan (Workplace Gender Equality Agency, 2022)[17]
- Globally, in 2021, 26% of all CEOs and managing directors were women (Catalyst, 2022)
- Globally, in 2020, 23% of executives and senior managers were women (Mercer, 2020)[18]
- In the EU, women make up almost half of all those employed (46.3%), yet among the largest publicly listed companies, only 20.2% of executives and 7.8% of CEOs are women (Eurostat, 2022)[19]
- 90% of companies worldwide had at least one woman in a senior management role as of 2021 (Catalyst, 2022)

Read that last statistic again because I don't know whether to laugh or cry. It's written in such a triumphant way. *One* woman, hurrah! The gender 'problem' is solved!

Clearly the progress is glacial. Based on 2020 trends, the global gender gap was not expected to be closed for another 100 years. Already a mammoth prospect, but according to new research from the World Economic Forum,[20] due to the Covid pandemic with women at the forefront of caring, the world is now going backwards on this long road to gender equality. The time required is now forecast at 136 years. I can't wait that long!

Lies, damn lies, and statistics

Looking closer to home in the UK, there have been 'gender celebrations' with the recent achievement of an all-time high of nearly 40% female representation in the boardroom. Since the government-backed Lord Davies Review started in 2011, urging British business to take female representation at senior levels more seriously, female ranks have swelled by some 30%.

But is this really the much-heralded 'sea change' for professional women? The statistics conceal a somewhat murkier picture. Less remarked on is the fact that most of the female positions around the executive table belong to non-executive directors (NEDs). That is, women who are members of the board of directors, but not executives of the company. Behind the statistics lies a plateauing number of full-time senior female executives, which has flatlined at around 11% for some 10 years. Professor Sue Vinnicombe, CBE, Founder Director of the Cranfield International Centre for Women Leaders, and co-author of the influential Female FTSE Board Report, tartly suggests, 'I am sure that all Chairs and CEOs of FTSE companies understand the business case for gender diversity at an intellectual level, but do they really believe in it and are they prepared to act on it?'[21]

Probably not, if the research from Bain & Co. mentioned above is representative of more than the 800 UK professionals already solicited. It's a great example of NIMBY-ism (Not In My Back Yard), with 79% of men believing gender parity in organizations is important, but only 48% seeing it as a strategic imperative. McKinsey, another global management consultancy doing excellent gender reporting, echo this sentiment. Gender parity is apparently important to men, just not *that* important!

Midlife myths in a man-made world

The 'Hampton-Alexander Review' was commissioned by the government to understand the reasons lying behind this persistent gender inequality at board level, and a range of FTSE 350 chairs and CEOs were asked for their opinion. As mentioned in the Introduction, it revealed a startling level of prejudice about female leaders, with some outrageous explanations.[22] For your delight, here are the top ten reasons:

1. 'I don't think women fit into a board environment'
2. 'There aren't that many women with the right credentials and depth of experience'
3. 'Most women don't want the hassle or pressure'
4. 'Shareholders just aren't interested in the make-up of the board, so why should we be?'
5. 'My other board colleagues wouldn't want to appoint a woman on our board'
6. 'All the good ones have been snapped up'
7. 'There aren't any vacancies at the moment. If there was, I'd think about a woman'
8. 'We need to build the pipeline from the bottom – there aren't enough senior women in this sector'
9. 'I can't just appoint a woman because I want to'

And my favourite coming in at #10:

10. 'We already have one thanks, so we're done. It's someone else's turn'

Dame Inga Beale's quote at the front of the Review speaks volumes:

> *Those women who have been a CEO in a large organisation will say, and in fact some will know, that our successors are going to be men. Speaking to several of them, the common view is that Chairs think they have done their bit by hiring a woman, now the role can go back to a man. It feels as though we took two steps forward and are now taking one step back.*[23]

Or, as one shrewd media commentator said, 'As you read these excuses, you might think it's 1918. Not 2018 when it was published. It reads like a comedy parody, not business for the 21st century.'[24]

Why it's easier to slay a dragon than kill a myth!

It's easy to smile wryly about the irony of some of these myths above. Well of course the women don't 'fit' around the board table when there's only one of them around! It becomes a much more sombre game when the stories become hard-nosed reality. As the research from Alison Konrad and Sumru Erkust makes clear, one female voice around the boardroom table equals the invisibility phase; two voices is the conspiracy phase; but three voices becomes the mainstream, 'It's normal to have women in the room and the problems go away.'[25] And it was clear in my study that once gender is combined with age and status, exclusion becomes an actuality.

And there are abundant scenarios of gender discrimination being played out again and again across our organizations today. Take Amanda Blanc, 55, the first female chief executive of Aviva (the UK's largest insurance company), subjected to a barrage of sexist comments at the company's first in-person AGM since the Covid pandemic. Investors intimated she was 'not the man for the job' or suggested she 'should be wearing trousers'. Posting on LinkedIn (May 2022), Blanc states,

> I guess that after you have heard the same prejudicial rhetoric for so long, it makes you a little immune to it all. I'd like to tell you that things have got better in recent years, but it's fair to say that it's actually increased. The more senior the role I've taken, the more overt the unacceptable behaviour.

Or take the case of Rachel Sutherland, 56, knitwear designer for high street UK fashion brand Superdry, awarded £96,000 in damages in 2022 after being passed over for promotion because of her age. During her time working for the retailer, Sutherland claimed she was repeatedly rejected for promotion in favour of less experienced colleagues and that she was forced to resign. A tribunal heard that bosses deemed her to be a 'low flight risk' and that she would stay 'no matter how she was treated' because of her age.[26]

Or take my recent excruciating evening facilitating a Q&A dinner with male board members, after leading an empowerment workshop for their female senior leaders. When these male board members were asked why they had just one female on the executive committee, the women were given the answer, 'We tried [to fill a recent leadership position]. We've asked the head-hunters, and the women just don't seem to exist.' Silence in the room, until one senior woman said, 'well, you didn't ask me?', followed by eight further voices, 'or me... or me...'.

Strangers within

This is the notion of exclusion just not being noticed or turning a blind eye to discrimination. My findings showed that the older woman is systemically excluded within the organization in three ways:

1. She is not young
2. She is not male
3. She is not always present (due to working part-time).

Heather Höpfl, who recently passed away, was a social scientist and feminist academic. Her writing strongly influenced me as she had a knack for pithily expressing – and understanding – the gender power structure in organizations. In her article, 'The lady vanishes', she suggests, 'Men do not realise the extent to which women live as strangers in their world. What is normal and taken for granted is a world which is defined, constructed, and maintained by male notions of order.'[27]

There are multiple conscious and unconscious ways women are excluded and it can take many forms. It's probable that male normative behaviour is so well established within the organization that the marginalization of the professional older woman is barely noticed, remarked on, or written about. Kristin, 53, an ex-human resources director, explains this well:

> *One of the phrases that always drives me nuts is when men talk about equality they say, 'yes, we need to level the playing field'. But what they're really talking about is football. That is, 'we've got to make sure you girls can play football'. But I don't want to play football, it's not my game, it's never going to play to my strengths and for me that's the fundamental bit that we're missing. This is the male paradigm that exists when we talk about diversity. What we're really trying to do in organizations is to squeeze everybody into a square box. And you go 'yes, but I'm round?' So essentially what we're being asked to do is alter our shape to fit into that box. That's what equality and diversity means to me as an older woman. It's trying to homogenize everyone to still fit the male system. Our processes have all been constructed by predominantly middle-class white men and therefore when you try and look at it from a different perspective it doesn't work. So, I think for me an inclusive paradigm would be recognizing that not everybody wants to play football, and not everybody wants to fit in a square box.*

The majority of my interviewees described either the scarcity of professional older women at the top of their companies, or their isolation as the sole representative of this age and gender within their organization. Such non-existence has been extensively researched and reported in the fashion and media industries, and my data echoed these findings, as Chris, a 56-year-old leader in a media company, suggests:

*There's virtually nobody in this company who is my age. If
anybody. I mean presumably somewhere there's somebody
my age but I'm not aware of them, so I can't say there's
nobody of my age, but I don't think I work with anybody
who is nearly my age.*

But the lack of visible older professional women in the
organizational field is, by no means, exclusive to the media
industry. Indeed, there was a distinct lack of senior middle-
aged female executives across many of my participants'
professions, including the professional services, the NHS,
and financial services, suggesting that the exclusion of
professional older women is not contained to a specific
industry. Jude is a good example. At 48, Jude is an executive
board director of a blue-chip insurance company, with
some 3,000 employees in the UK. She could picture few
professional women of her age in the organization:

*I think about the people who sit round the table with
me, there are no other ladies. Not one. And in the level
below me there is probably 3 out of 40 or 50. It's a really
male environment. Most women are in the call centres,
there are a few in HR and a couple in finance who do the
accounts but at lower-level roles. There is only me on the
Executive Committee.*

Whilst Jude's comment corroborates the research that
older women are confined to lower status levels within
organizations, genuine thought was given by interviewees
to the numbers of higher status women over 45 within their
organization. There was a characteristic struggle to recall
numbers, as Meera (in professional services) said: 'I can't
think of any senior woman at the top of our company, maybe
one… yeah, I could find out how many we've got globally,
but I can't think of any?'

There has always been a historical silencing of women's voices through the use of status and silence and certainly respondents discussed women of their age in lower positions of power, with men as 'Heads' and women as 'Deputies', as Niamh, a teaching professional, discussed: 'For a profession that is massively dominated by females there are relatively few female heads and you know, the old glass ceiling thing is true in schools – you get lots of female deputies.'

The 'backslappy boys club'

The male paradigmatic organization, with boardrooms, leadership channels, and networking opportunities dominated by men, is well evidenced and further echoed in my study. For the women I interviewed, 'normality' was having a male boss, with three-quarters of interviewees having a male line manager. Fifty per cent of the organizations had fewer than five female leaders in their entire company. Only three women had a female boss, two of whom were the CEO, and both of whom set up their organizations. (Interestingly, within these latter five companies, there was gender parity or female dominance at executive level.) The dominant male presence, voice and male metaphors were present in conversations and the majority grip of patriarchal power showed little sign of release.

What is key to this book is the manifestation of this male paradigm. At one extreme were the stories offered of bullying and the acceptance of bullying in the culture, and at the other extreme is simply isolation. Dionne's experience was by no means the only example. Dionne, 52, is a senior manager within the civil service and one of the few female leaders in a male-dominant culture:

If I go through all of the leaders, percentage-wise it is mainly male. They're not bad guys, they're just very matey. It's boys locker room talk the whole time, football and so on. They disappear through dinner to somebody's room because a game is on and stuff like that. They're just thoughtless and not particularly welcoming. They don't accept me as one of them and it's obvious in the boardroom because when I say something, they ignore me or it's just hard to get heard. It's a pretty exhausting environment to work in.

Or there are examples of isolation, as Jude further mentions, of not having female 'mates' around the leadership table:

It feels strange being the only woman. Silly things like last week when I felt emotional. Nobody noticed, or would have cared, even if I had come in sobbing it would have passed everyone by. Before [the new CEO] joined, the Exco was totally male, and it was common to be rude about women, is she blonde? Can she type? It was just awful. But there is nobody you can have a decent, personal conversation with here at the top, no one you can discuss your tough day with, because they simply don't have these conversations. It's a backslappy boys club. So it's an interesting environment but it'll be tough for us to recruit women into the senior team because there are no levels below in the female pipeline, so we'll have to recruit them in.

Your time is up!

As long as discriminatory language or practice is neither considered abhorrent by individuals nor disabled by the organization, the more the subtleties and nuance behind the maintenance of power are accepted. And this acceptance can give rise to a surrender to the status quo, or, worse, relinquishing one's role in the organization. At least five women I interviewed discussed the signals, sometimes nuanced and sometimes overt, that their 'time was up'. Respondents discussed the sense of feeling 'sidelined', with projects quietly going elsewhere, and that, as the past, they could not be part of the organizational future. Sandra, 64, a leader in the media industry, articulated this powerfully:

> *People felt very strongly round me that there was a new view in the organization that older women didn't have a place in this organization and that I sort of stuck out like a sore thumb, and that I should just fall on my sword. I should just move on you know, what was I still doing there?*

We met Kristin briefly earlier (and you'll meet her further in Chapter 7). A 53-year-old human resources director, who recently resigned to do a PhD, she describes the sensation after she left her role:

> *The message was clear, 'if you've got corporate memory, it's time to go, this place belongs to the young'. So, there was an undertone that as a 50-year-old woman you weren't in the core demographic, you were past your 'sell by date' and there was this not-so-subtle message 'that you need to move on'. The irony is my (male) boss is older than me, and still there! By the time I left the executive team, there was only one woman left. The other three had left citing reasons of not being valued, not feeling fulfilled and a sense of 'I know I can do more, I've got lots more to offer'.*

It is also possible that the isolation for professional older women, the lack of role models and the surprise they are still 'in the game' is one of the reasons that many of the respondents could not conceive of themselves in a senior position. Nina is one of many interviewees who intends to step up, but seems almost puzzled by the idea of taking a senior position, 'Someone did say would you go the next level? Interesting I have never thought of it, I have just written it off, I never thought I'd get this far again.'

Nina is a 54-year-old business leader in an international retail company and what she is describing is very common. 'If you can't see it, you can't be it', has been the rallying cry for female role models, but this scarcity also has a more insidious impact. The 'stereotype embodiment theory'[28] might be a mouthful but remains one of my pet theories. With her theory, Becca Levy proposed that people absorb stereotypes from their surrounding culture, which then (positively or negatively) affect their functioning and health. Ergo, you internalize society's expectation of an older woman, and that becomes your self-fulfilling prophecy. Put another way, we become what we expect to become.

And women are acutely aware of this. Indeed, they offer palpable frustration at the apparent limitations and myths surrounding older women and an astute awareness of the damage this can cause, not only to the individual, but also to the broader societal and cultural perception of, and action towards, older professional women. Gaynor, a 57-year-old academic, is clear in her belief that the 'decline narrative' can instil women at midlife with a limited mindset: 'I think there is a lot of challenging to be done which is actually you don't have to do that, you don't have to be like that, you have choices.' And she further explains:

> *I don't believe memory declines with age, I don't think physical capability declines with age, not at the rate that people would have you believe, I don't think motivation declines either, which is where I get to with the self-fulfilling prophecy thing – which is if you say to yourself, I'm over 50 therefore I can't or shouldn't, then you won't.*

Silence and the last taboo?

Perhaps easier said than done? When I listen back to some of my interviews, there's a wistful regret of embodying such expectations. Take Patricia, 60, a university professor who summarizes this with astuteness.

I think what I am trying to say is that within the wider culture there is something that is encouraged and makes us as older women withdraw. Have lower expectations. Keep quiet. Not expect to be noticed. Be unassertive. So, it is not that the university is promoting older women, it is simply not talked about.

Patricia's comment has stayed with me – 'simply not talked about'. Essentially, the disappearance of middle-aged women from our organizations is enabled through silence – systemically as well as individually. As Mary Evans, a political and social commentator, suggests in her book, *The Persistence of Gender Inequality*,[29] the closer the woman gets to power, the more urgent the need to put them down.

Sandra, 64, is an advocate for gender and age equality within her industry and unafraid to call out what she perceives as 'transgressive behaviour'. She offered dramatic examples of being routinely silenced with 'uncontrollable hysterical rage' from her boss due to her willingness to bring out into the open issues of ageism, sexism and the menopause without an organizational remit. She further suggests her organization, and the media industry at large, 'turns a blind eye' to the departure of professional older women:

I don't think they even recognize that it's a problem for them, they're quite happy for them (older women) to leave, it's not a problem for them. 'Oh, that's good they've gone, we can bring in another one.' I know really good women who are no longer working, and I think, so did they just have nothing left to offer? It's the lack of imagination that's shocking and a waste to society.

And it is possible that the culture of silence experienced within many organizations is reflective of society, which encourages older women to remain quiet and keep their expectations low. Kristin, previously an HR director who still leads the way in diversity, particularly for older women, agrees that issues of 'taboo' lie at the heart of the silence:

> *I can only assume that it's because we don't fit into a male paradigm, and it's either that we've got no relevance as older women, or that it's a bit squeamish and we don't want to talk about it. I would say even mental health, which is supposedly the last taboo, is being talked about more than older women's issues, so actually I would say that we're the last taboo.*

In conclusion, I'd venture that just as women are reaching the age when they are coming into their own, realizing their confidence, upping their leadership game, and asserting their power, their hold on the management rungs becomes more slippery and the prejudice much louder. Perhaps the myths perpetuated above are just convenient social stories that serve to maintain the male-dominated organization, at a time when women are in a position to progress in a significant way? Or perhaps it's just too easy to maintain the status quo through turning a blind eye to the problem, sidelining the issue, or creating stories that place the blame for the problem firmly and squarely back in the hands of the individual.

As we move forwards in this story, the invisible thread that remains undiscussed in most of the gender debates, books, reports, government commissions, or podcasts is that of age. Or more specifically, ageism and gendered ageism. Critical really, as it is age that's the clandestine backdrop to key decisions and divisions in the workplace, and when age is interwoven with gender (and further with race or class), the issue ramps up to a whole new level!

CHAPTER 2

AGEING IN THE WORKPLACE

Age is a potent organizer of our lifespace, and power accrues to those who are able to shape age cultures and control the age agenda.
(Professor Stephen Fineman, *Organizing Age*)[1]

It's pretty brutal for anyone to age in the workplace. You're on the way down, not up – and organizations prop up this message with clear branding representing their youthful vitality. Marry older age with being female and the situation is particularly corrosive, the so-called 'double whammy' of gendered ageism.[2] It's not just the off the cuff banter (like congratulating me on my 'bravery' for displaying my natural white hair at a presentation I was delivering, or offering me an afternoon nap), nor the hours spent in the washroom trying to prop up my bags and sags! What I mean is that with middle age twinned with decline, the message is clear – prove yourself, you're not relevant anymore. In this chapter, we'll dive deeper into what it is like to get older at work, and understand how, in the light of ageism, the older man still manages to swim effortlessly to the top of the organization, whilst the older woman paddles furiously to get to the surface.

Don't dare to get old

In the UK, we have abolished the mandatory retirement age, increased the state pension age, and introduced age discrimination legislation. But despite such manifold policies declaring a war on ageism in the workplace, it is alive and kicking in workplaces, from filmsets to forecourts, from headquarters to hospitals. This is not necessarily deliberate, as discrimination happens implicitly as often as it is explicit – but once noticed, it is hard to not see. For example, the active and youthful orientation of a company starts with the apprentice and graduate training schemes, showing young people laughing their way into a career. Posters favour the 'fit and healthy' (i.e. younger workers), with older people often depicted in pharmaceutical or hospital settings as the 'patient'. Casual 'banter' paints the 'baby boomer' stealing all of the money, or the older worker being put out to pasture. Training schemes for the middle-aged are either non-existent or focused on your pension and retirement options. The language of ambition, career options, moving up, motivation, and energy belongs to youth. Also, it is not that organizations are ignoring gender issues – far from it, as most interviewees in my study were able to recall a litany of diversity, flexibility, and training policies within their organizations. But they reported that existing policies are geared towards either attracting a new generation of employees, improving gender balance, or helping women return to work after maternity leave.

Recent headlines begging the over-50s to return to the workplace post-pandemic (we've even been given a name, Generation 50, so you know it's a 'thing'!) are too little, too late.[3] Not only were the over-50s 'retired early' during the pandemic, with older women hit the hardest, but it comes after decades of doom-laden business headlines declaring war on the older worker. Business literature contributed to this with articles using apocalyptic language, including the 'silver tsunami', the 'demographic time bomb' and the 'perfect storm of the demographic risk', with the ageing workforce persistently viewed through a prism of complication and difficulty.[4] Little surprise that Dorothy Byrne, President of Murray Edwards College, Cambridge

University, sharply retorted, in response to such headlines, 'we older people want to work. But bosses just don't want us to. The discrimination we face is an outrage.'[5]

And participants in my study echoed the research. For example, few organizations are as explicitly age discriminatory as the examples offered from the respondents working within the professional service industry. Meera, a 51-year-old HR leader, revealed statistics in her firm that show the average age of workers is 27, with some 80% of the workforce being under 45, and an 'engagement agreement' that ensures all partners (of both sexes) exit before they are 55 years of age. The latter is so that the firm can 'offer partnership opportunities to our talent'. The message to Meera is clear:

> *I haven't had a pay rise for a number of years, and I get bonuses, but the base pay hasn't changed. I've sort of had the message that you're really well paid, you're not worth much more to us, your career isn't going up and we have a food chain to feed of junior people.*

Stephen Fineman, Professor Emeritus in Organizational Behaviour at the School of Management, University of Bath, and author of *Organizing age*, confirms the stress on youth being the 'productive and aesthetic icons of capitalism's projects'.[6] His comments were lent weight in my research, with women commenting that the notion of youth is associated with positive qualities, such as energy, creativity, fun and wellness. This is despite many women believing that the younger people within their organizations did not deliver a return on investment, and, as one respondent, Min, says, 'they push forwards and absorb the oxygen'. The presumption that 'talent' equals 'youth' was confirmed in particular by the human resource/people leaders I interviewed. They discussed in multiple ways an 'obsession with youth' in their organizations and the propulsion to bring young people in through graduate and apprenticeship training schemes, 'feeding the food chain' from the bottom up.

Despite the Equality Act of 2010 outlawing age discrimination, it is significant that only one interviewee could recall a policy held by their organization that positively benefits her generation. Age, and ageism, are ignored. Meera described her company's ageist policy as 'intolerable' and 'head in the sand' and further explained her endeavours to persuade her company to sign up to an ageing workforce policy:

> I attend this 'Age at Work' forum, so as members we've obsessively signed up to this target to increase our 'over-50' workforce by 12%. I've done a paper on how we can do that and there's a few of us sitting on it, but we can't find the route into our leadership to make this a priority for them.

One particularly insightful comment, from Sandra, summarized the situation for many of the respondents:

> If you're the past, you can't be the present or the future.

Age is (not) just a number!

From the moment we breathe, it is age that tells you when it's appropriate to sit, walk, eat solids, and talk. Your age decrees when you'll start school, sit exams, and enjoy college. In your 20s there will be multiple messages that now is a good time to think about getting married, and in your 30s to sort out your career and your kids. By your 40s it's all about strive, juggle, c'mon achieve, time is running out! And so the notion that 'age is just a number' seems to be a romantic and extravagant understatement!

But there is a change in expectation once you hit midlife. The talk starts about retirement (as soon as you hit 50), pensions (or the lack of them), ageing bodily woes and parental care (welcome to Chapter 6), but overall, there is a gentle message that you are becoming invisible and no longer important to the workplace or society. Just look at the plethora of online forms. Age? 0–18; 18–30; 31–40; 41–50; 51+. And that's where it stops. Suddenly you are part of a homogeneous, over-50, 'mass'.

Routinely ignored in much of the literature surrounding ageing, lifespans, and adult development, midlife is a phase of life that is wrapped up in myths and riddled with assumptions. Described as the 'last uncharted territory' of the life course, there are midlife scientists, such as Margaret Gullette, urging that our attitude to midlife, seeing this time of the 'life course' as a time of deterioration, needs to become the biggest story of our time.[7] In her many inspiring books, including *Aged by Culture* and *Declining to Decline*, she urged readers to understand that much of what we dread about ageing is actually the result of ageism, which we can, and should, battle as strongly as we do racism, sexism, and other forms of bigotry. She states, 'the truth is that aging-into-the-middle-years, or even aging-past-youth, can be better or worse depending on social context. Historical forces produce waves of decline. We have been enduring a tidal wave.'

She makes a great point. With life expectancy today in the western world around 80 years (higher for women), anyone in their mid-40s has as many productive years ahead of them as behind them. This thought sometimes blows me away. At 59 years of age, I still have a potential 20-year career ahead of me. Woohoo! The things I can do with this. But you only have to take a brief twirl through the card shop to know that this is not what society, or the workplace, has planned for me, with our later years twinned with decline. Somewhere around the age of 50, you'll start receiving the birthday cards declaring that you're now either over the hill, or on the slippery slope downwards – with drink, cake, or shopping being your only lasting saviours (they have a point!). It seems that social expectations for midlife are based on a life expectancy that is more in tune with how we lived 40 years ago, when someone in their 70s was 'a good age' and the healthier ones among them could go for a short walk.

Crisis, what crisis?

Where did this persistent, ageist, decline story come from? Of course there are complex and far-reaching historical and societal influences at play here, but to understand how we got to this present state of affairs, it's worth taking a brief diversion towards the so-called 'midlife crisis'. How could I avoid these two words that are still stubbornly embedded in our everyday language? Over the course of a few years in the 20th century, the midlife crisis went from being an obscure psychological theory to an all-embracing phenomenon – expanded to include practically any inner strife. Unhappy with your job; your marriage; your health; your kids? Aged somewhere between 40 and 65? Yup, that's your midlife crisis! Divorce, have an affair, change your family. Buy the Ferrari, the bike, the boat (or, modern man, the motorhome!), and calm will be restored to your life.

The architect of the midlife crisis never meant it to be this way. Coined in 1957 by the Canadian psychoanalyst and social scientist, Elliott Jaques, he used this phrase to describe a lengthy depressive period experienced by people in their mid-30s. He studied great (male) painters and noticed that, at this age, men experienced symptoms such as a sudden inability to enjoy life, hypochondriacal concerns over health and appearance, and compulsive attempts to remain young. His subsequent 1965 paper, 'Death and the midlife crisis', hit the zeitgeist, leaping from academia to popular culture – so much so, that the midlife crisis, which had barely existed five or six years before, was suddenly treated like a biological inevitability.[8] He watched in amazement at the avalanche of interest, describing this notion to an interviewer as a 'tiny little piece of work' and urging others to look at his later work (they didn't).[9] Interestingly, over the course of his own long life, his work shifted from being about midlife, to later life, stating at the age of 83, 'you can count on reaching your peak somewhere between 90 and 120, and I don't mean that as a joke'.

Research findings countering this overwhelming sense of midlife calamity have largely fallen on deaf ears. In the largest known study of people enjoying midlife in the US, MIDUS,[10] scientists found that a crisis in midlife simply didn't exist, with the vast majority of 'midlifers' being healthy, with busy social lives and at the earning peak of their careers. Moreover, it showed that people have crises throughout their lives, not just in midlife, more likely related to a life event, such as a health problem, job loss, or a divorce, not to ageing. Indeed, a quarter-life crisis at 25 was much more likely!

The language of gendered ageism[11]

So, if ageing executives are facing decline and discrimination, how come our boardrooms and our leadership teams are in the powerful grip of white, middle-aged men? I can hear you shouting that from here! In 2019, British feminist, author and activist, Caroline Criado Perez, exposed in her book, *Invisible Women: Data Biases in a World Designed for Men*, the consequences of gender disparities in a male-dominated society.[12] From the size of toilets, the design of seatbelts and the medical profession's dismissal of women's stated symptoms, Perez showed the danger to life and happiness that comes from just being a woman. And midlife is no different. According to statistics from the AARP[13] (America's largest non-profit organization dedicated to researching the lives of the over-50s), 64% of women say they have been the target of, or witnessed, age discrimination. Yet only 3% of older women have ever made a complaint to a supervisor, human resource person, another organization or government agency. Writing in the *Chicago Tribune*, journalist Bonnie Marcus says, 'beyond the headlines of celebrated older women in the spotlight right now, there's a tribe of older women in the workplace who have lost their jobs due to ageism and sexism. These women suffer in silence as they are marginalized, passed over or pushed out.'[14] Progressing from the #MeToo movement, Bonnie suggests a new hashtag of #notdoneyet.

But why precisely are middle-aged women subject to gendered ageism in a way that men aren't? This leads us to an inescapable conversation about the 'problem' of the female ageing body in the workplace, which gets us closer to understanding how gendered ageism has quietly flourished in the workplace. For decades, there has been research and public talk about the discrimination against the younger female reproductive body. That is, if I hire a woman, what if she has a baby? Do we want to afford maternity pay? And what if she doesn't return? And what if she gets too emotional? How much easier to hire a man. And of course a woman doesn't need to have an actual baby to feel the weight of judgement – she simply has to hold the *potential* for reproduction in her body.

So welcome to the older woman – no periods, no problem! Wishful thinking, it seems. Whilst the older male body is linked with fine wines, eligible bachelors, or silver foxes, all kind of sexy and interesting, the best the older woman can hope for is to be labelled a cougar. More likely, the older woman is labelled a hag, crone, harridan, mutton, old bag, witch, bint, battle-axe, frump, matron, spinster, I'm on a roll!

Indeed, I'm struggling to think of a single respectful word to describe a woman over 50.

And if these seem like isolated words, or 'not in my workplace', the illustrations of pejorative language used in the workplace towards my interviewees might give you pause for thought. Littered with sexist and ageist overtones, the women I talked to had been called all sorts of names from 'blocker... also ran... older bird... old biddy' through to 'frigid old cow... older aunt... throwback... fuddy duddy'. Why is language so important? Lori, a 50-year-old talent director, whom you'll meet more in Chapter 4, describes an example of a recent interview process where the language and image of the older woman influence the hiring process:

> We hired an HR director into one of our business lines and there was an internal candidate, who was a woman, and I thought would have been brilliant. She's 50 and the discussion was, 'well you know it's not that she would not be good at the job', everyone could see that she'd be good at the job, but 'she'll be a blocker' and 'this will be her last gig', and 'where's she going to go next?' and 'we're not kind of elevating the game through putting her in it'. So, we went outside, and we hired a guy who was one year younger, 49.

Nina, 54, was concerned that her younger colleagues had recently called her a 'fuddy duddy who doesn't move with the times'. And Bel describes a conversation with a fellow male director that highlights the anomaly of attractive older women with the sentence, 'You know, for an older bird, you're quite attractive.' Bel is a 50-year-old property manager, and in rebutting a sexual advance, Bel was accused of being a 'frigid old cow, I didn't realise you bat for the other side'. Whilst I'm writing this book and re-reading my interviews, I notice in my transcripts that much of this language was relayed back to me with a resigned shrug or a laugh (never fury or indignation), and I know this response is the outcome of years of older women being 'othered' within organizations. That is, through the use of humour, or resignation, exclusion is normalized within so many organizations, embedded in language and practice. Ageism, as defined by author and activist Ashton Applewhite,[15]

> *occurs when a dominant group uses its power to oppress or exploit or silence or simply ignore people who are much older or significantly younger. We experience ageism any time someone assumes we're 'too old' for something – be it a task, a relationship, or a haircut, instead of finding out who we are and what we're capable of.*

Losing your 'erotic capital'?

And so the language of gendered ageism contributes to the maintenance of the powerful male paradigm. But alongside language come looks. And the research is very clear. As men age, they are viewed as more competent and valuable in the workplace; as women age, they lose their credibility with every new wrinkle.[16] The message is consistent: Looks matter. Age matters.

Take Dame Mary Beard's appearance on *Question Time*, a British political TV panel show, which prompted an outpouring of misogyny.[17] A 60-year-old Cambridge scholar, Professor Beard had the audacity to appear on TV with no make-up and unpinned long grey hair. Web posts discussed her pubic hair ('does she brush the floor with it?'), whether she needed 'rogering' (that comment was taken down, as was the speculation about the capaciousness of her vagina, and the plan to plant a d*** in her mouth). Many of the postings were aggressive and sexual and included a photo of her face superimposed onto a picture of female genitalia. Explaining why she was refusing to laugh off the comments, Mary Beard wrote:

First, the misogyny here is truly gobsmacking. The whole c*** talk, and the kind of stuff represented by the photo is more than a few steps into sadism. It would be quite enough to put many older women off appearing in public, contributing to political debate, especially as all of this comes up on Google.

In 2010, British social scientist and Professor at the London School of Economics, Catherine Hakim, raised feminist hackles by coining the notion of 'erotic capital',[18] which, in a nutshell, is the supposed power that accrues to those with a combination of beauty, social skills, good dress sense, physical fitness, liveliness, sex appeal, and sexual competence. And while it can be exploitable by all, Hakim argued that young women have more scope to manipulate it in the workplace seeing as men want sex more than women. Of course, arguments raged on all sides! But she has a point. Once youth is equated with energy, creativity, and success, and female ageing with incompetence and irrelevance, the corporate expectation for the older woman is clear. Do not *look* old, and do not *act* old. And midlife women know the game. Serious amounts of time, money and energy are expended on looking and acting young, staying innovative and distancing themselves from any ageing stereotypes.

Let's start with the unsurprising thread running through many of these interviews about the need to show control over one's body, particularly when control equals competence. This is explicitly affirmed by Gaynor:

You don't have to appear young and pretty, that's not a pre-requisite. But I think as an older woman you certainly have to appear to look fit and confident. You have to show you're in control of your body, because that gives the impression that you're in control of your intellectual age and your competence.

And the seriousness with which Gaynor, 57, believes age is equated with ineffectiveness has led to her presenting herself as seven years younger than she is. An administrative error enabled this, and she has not corrected it, for, as she says: 'If age could be a barrier to my advancement in my career, then I care about my age. I think the image of a 60-year-old plus woman is incompetent, past it.'

What we are facing is the conclusion that the older female body is both invisible – in that it is no longer seen – and hypervisible – in that it is all that is seen. At every interview, women discussed their self-presentation in the workplace and the strenuous efforts they took to 'act younger'. Here Nina presents the need to focus on energy: 'I never say I'm tired at work, I never say it. The young people all do, but I keep things like that to myself. I am conscious of not appearing old.'

With a focus on youth, conversations ranged from hair, skin, make-up, nails, clothes, shoes, to diet, weight, and exercise. For example, Ana, a 54-year-old managing director of a legal firm, dyes her hair, has skin tightening, gel nails, a personal trainer, a rigorous diet, and a daily weigh-in. Her interview was representative of the lengths many of the women are going to in order to discipline their body, often alongside their disciplined life: 'I see a personal trainer twice a week, I wear a Fitbit, I try to do 10,000 steps a day and I go on my indoor bike for 20 minutes every morning.' In her book, *How to Age*,[19] Anne Karpf neatly summarizes this sensation of ageing: 'Although we're living longer, fitter and healthier lives than ever before, we spend more time worrying about ageing; we get older later but fear getting older younger.'

With a focus on showing up as relevant and up-to-date, the embodied presence of the older women in the workplace was more acute for those women surrounded by younger people in their environment – for example, media, fashion, schools, and universities. The desire (and need) to 'fit in' in this context had a more anxious edge. Chris, 56, a senior figure in advertising, discussed being in an organization where she was one of the oldest women there:

> *It's tough knowing you are always facing people who are younger than you. I never thought I'd feel old, but lately I hate looking in the mirror. Am I going to look old-fashioned, do I look on brand? Or do I just look like a middle-aged woman who's trying to look as if she's on brand? Who am I kidding? I want to be engaging, I want to be interesting, I want to be relevant.*

In a similar vein, the urge to avoid age stereotyping, and 'push against the boundaries of what is expected of a woman of my age', was keenly expressed by Kristin:

> *I want to prove to myself, and probably to other people, that actually being in your 50s doesn't define you… so I've run marathons, I've climbed Kilimanjaro, I've done 100-mile bike rides and it's as much as anything to prove that I'm physically fitter than people half my age. So, there was a little bit of 'right I'm going to show the lot of you'.*

However, this need to prove oneself physically took a much darker turn when women discussed the lengths they went to to ensure that they did not present an ageing, sick, or frail body within the workplace. Frances has recently recovered from pneumonia, having 'worked myself into a frazzle', and both Bel and Raya have ME (myalgic encephalomyelitis), caused, they believe, by the stress of work and, critically, the need to cover it up:

> *I was so worried, because I don't want to look like I'm not pulling my weight, and in the end the ME just made it an added pressure. I don't want to be written off as someone who can't hack the pace here. So, I over-compensated and*

made myself sick which is why I ended up with ME in the first place really.

And so the standards of our culture seem to create more problems for women than men as they move through their middle and later years. In contrast to the confident, 'seen and heard' older man, visible signs of age can erode a woman's status, with women under pressure to maintain a youthful appearance, outlook, and body. In other words, how you look is linked to how you will be judged, with power landing in the hands of those who are taken the most seriously. How this happens to be male hands rather than female hands is a long historical tale, summarized in the next chapter.

CHAPTER 3

THE INVISIBLE FORCE
FIELD OF HISTORY

We groan under centuries of cultural baggage.
(Louise Foxcroft, *Hot Flushes, Cold Science*)[1]

How on earth did the female body, whether young or old, become such an easy target for maintaining power and political control? There are two ways in which power is maintained within the male-controlled organization, that is, (a) by maintaining the status quo at all costs, and (b) by weakening the opposition. And historical theories about the female body have been used successfully over the centuries as a means to achieve both of these aims. But particularly used against the middle-class, middle-aged women, who were most at risk of challenging the patriarchal status quo, and whose bodies had to be shown as feeble and inferior.

As history tends to repeat itself, we'll consider its long attitudinal shadow. If you read the literature surrounding the medicalization of the female body from the Ancient Greeks through to the current day, it is not hard to reach the conclusion that, throughout history, the female body has been used as a weapon for political gain, profit, and social control.[2] And so we have to look backwards first (a brief anatomical and feminist history lesson, I promise!), in order to look forwards and deepen our understanding about present attitudes towards older female executives.

The inferior female body: the Ancient Greeks

Whilst much of the feminist literature regarding the medicalization of women's bodies considers the early Victorian days as the turning point for the male domination of female health, women have been stigmatized as biologically inferior since the Ancient Greeks.[3] The Greeks were keen to put women in the category of less than human. This was something very important for that society – part of the deep need to understand the world. So their philosophy kept women (and children and slaves) as being closer to animals than to men. The writings of Aristotle and Galen formed the basis of 'scientific' discussion on women's bodies from the 4th century BC through to the 18th century, with their theories focusing on the concept of heat, which was of primary importance to the Hippocratic school of thought. Because men's reproductive organs were outside of their body, they were considered warmer and superior. As women's organs were considered to be a reversal of the male organs, yet located inside their bodies, they were considered cooler animals, with only those embryos with sufficient heat being able to develop into fully human form – the male form. The rest became female, otherwise known as 'monstrosities', considered less than fully formed and literally half-baked. From this ancient starting point, the male body was considered the norm and the female an inferior version of it.[4]

Not so enlightened

The inverted female organs were re-drawn by Da Vinci in the 15th century and repeated by Vesalius in the 16th century – widely regarded as the founder of modern anatomy. Despite rejecting the ancient view that sex differences pervade the body, Vesalius accepted that the female reproductive organs were 'imperfect, inverted and internal' and therefore inferior.[5] Whilst there were stirrings of a challenge to women's supposed inferiority by the mid-17th century, with some scientists arguing that women might be considered 'completely human' (god forbid!), this movement was small and overwhelmed by the Age of Enlightenment in the 18th century.

Eighteenth-century anatomy depicted women with smaller skulls, arguing this provided evidence of the subordinate position of women in European society and women's inferior intellectual capabilities. Londa Schiebinger, a scholar of 18th-century anatomy, writes,

> *this scientific measure of women's lesser 'natural reason' was used to buttress arguments against women's participation in the public spheres of government and commerce, science, and scholarship. The larger female pelvis was used in parallel fashion to prove that women were naturally destined for motherhood, the confined sphere of hearth and home.*[6]

Her illustrations of female anatomy in the book, *The Making of the Modern Body*, might not be the first book you'd give someone at Christmas, but I love it!

Victorian: early and late

With the rise of capitalism and industrialism, an important shift took place to ensure women continued to be seen as too weak or, later, too moral. Such 'proven' anatomical facts of difference, used to prescribe different roles for men and women in the social hierarchy, therefore stepped up a gear in the Victorian era as women became strongly associated with their irrational, unstable bodies, and men with their rational, stable minds.[7] Echoes of today! Influential philosophers joined with anatomists in strengthening the growing association of masculinity with reason and science, and femininity with feeling and the moral sphere of the home. With the ascent of science, the professionalization of medicine and the exclusion of female midwives from their traditional birthing role, women were firmly placed out of reach of status, power, and control.[8] By 1842, legislation prevented much industrial labour for women and girls, justified on the grounds of public health. The framework for gendered employment legislation started here: as the female body was believed to be biologically unstable, women could not be treated in the same way as able-bodied men. This world view can be seen, in the words of American author and political activist Barbara Ehrenreich, to proceed 'from the market, from the realm of the economic, or public life. It was by its nature external to women, capable of seeing them only as aliens.'[9]

During this period of the late 19th century, there was an obsessive concern with women as 'organs of reproduction'.[10] And it is no coincidence. As women demanded to move into the public sphere, so the response was to emphasize the private sphere and women's unique role in reproduction. From the 1850s, this was a time of intense feminist agitation and the 'woman question' an ongoing social crisis. During the decades from 1870 to 1910, middle-class women were beginning to organize on behalf of higher education, entrance to the professions and political rights. And simultaneously, claims regarding the female nervous disorders of anorexia nervosa, hysteria, and neurasthenia became epidemic. Importantly, each time women were creeping up a rung of power, the claims surrounding their supposedly 'sick' bodies became louder.

But women continued to contradict the 'cult' of true womanhood and their supposed inferiority in the public sphere. The feminist challenge was sweeping, embracing education and occupation, and challenging their legal, political, and social status. With the passing of the 1882 Married Women's Property Act and the opening of higher education, the path was laid for the creation of the nationwide suffrage movement. Women were prising open the gates of power – or rather, being chained to them.

The female body: in the warzone

Scientists responded to this unrest with a detailed and sustained examination of the differences between men and women that justified their differing, unequal, social roles. Centuries-old evidence regarding the conservation of energy, sexual selection, physiological differences, and the frailty of the female reproductive body was reworked – theories to ensure women remained inferior and subservient to the natural order. Through anatomy and physiology, evolutionary biology, physical anthropology, psychology and sociology, scientists evolved comprehensive theories of sexual difference.[11] Notice the number of scientists concerned with maintaining the world order! As the 20th century dawned, neurologists entered into this debate. Not only was Dr Charles L. Dana anxious 'that the upper half of the female spinal cord was a little on the light side for politics',[12] but brain scientists infamously proposed that women's intellectual inferiority stemmed from their smaller and lighter brains, becoming known as 'the missing five ounces of the female brain'.[13] The doctrine of female inferiority was preached from the pulpits, exclaimed from the lecterns, and written up in books.[14] Anything to justify the existing disparities of the sex roles. Men's lives would be immensely complicated by any abdication of women from the sanctuary of the home. Moreover, the stability of the established social order appeared at risk. Hence women's derogation of duty was not just personal but political and societal. Morally, however, women had been transformed from being sick, as claimed in the early religious tracts, to being morally superior. If sickness was losing its hold, morality might just work better! Upheld as 'sexually perfect', Charles Darwin lauded women's 'greater tenderness and less selfishness' as opposed to men's 'ambition which passes too easily into selfishness'.[15] Women's distinctive moral qualities, those of feeling and instinct, permitted men to 'benevolently' enable women to fulfil their natural destiny as mothers and conservators of custom in the confined sphere of home. Nothing was as important as motherhood, or as President Roosevelt told a gathering of women in 1908: 'The good mother, the wise mother is more important to the community than even the ablest man, her career is worthier of honor and is more useful to the community than the career of any man, no matter how successful.' Authoritatively, he urged women to do their duty as wife and mother, earning 'the right to our contempt' should they shirk such moral duty.[16]

Despite the granting of suffrage after the First World War (in some but not all countries) and the growth of women's international activism, historians agree that there was a highly conservative reaction against feminist goals in the interwar years.[17] This changed as women were thrust back into work during the Second World War, with over seven million women involved in war work at its peak. It became inevitable that women had their horizons limited as the war ended. With the dawn of the postwar era and men demobilized, western economies faced a crisis, with both the US and British governments needing to counter fears that soldiers would return to an employment market saturated by women. Women's 'moral duty' was again called to the fore, urging women back into the home and prompting them towards marriage, childrearing, and homemaking.[18]

Medicalizing the older woman: the 1950s

Up until this point, the stress on the inferiority of the female body was aimed at all ages. But in the 1950s, society was dealing with a fresh female problem – women living longer and working until retirement heralded a new threat to the status quo. The older woman who, past childrearing years, was in a position to return to work and climb up the greasy pole of power. The political and social directive was clear – she should be halted! And so, for the middle-aged woman, the 1950s were the dawn of a new age where medical views and cultural circumstances converged to create a climate in which female ageing became the target for powerful discrimination. History replayed itself and the realization was clear: if the middle-aged woman was perceived as 'sick' (it worked in the Victorian days), she would be unable or unwilling to grab power. Menopause was the obvious target – being the only biological difference between men and women.[19] Full-page advertising campaigns for oestrogen products ran repeatedly in the newspapers depicting menopausal women as 'mercurial and capricious'. Abbott, a pharmaceutical company, ran an infamous advertisement for its Estrone (an oestrogen product) showing a drawing of an older woman weeping over a sketch of herself at a younger age, 'the girl *she* left behind'. The message was clear – older women were vulnerable, distressed, and incapable of dealing with their jobs – and in need of help. The imagery used in the advertisements is significant, with older women portrayed as physically unattractive, tense, anxious, and irritable – a negative drain on their husbands. 'It's no easy thing for a man to take the stings and barbs of business life', claimed one ad, 'then to come home to the turmoil of a woman going through the change of life'. In another, a photograph of a bus driver featured alongside one of an angry female passenger, with the headline: 'He is suffering from estrogen deficiency. She is the reason why.'

But the real competition in the 1950s and 1960s came from manufacturers of sedatives, who began to advertise their drugs for the relief of menopausal symptoms, promising to relieve depression, anxiety, and restore self-esteem.[20] Phyllosan was the 'fortifying' drug of choice for the over-40s. I asked my 94-year-old mum about this. 'Oh yes', she said, 'we all took it'. You'll love the wording for the Phyllosan advertisement:

Husband: 'Still ironing at this time of night, mother? Don't you think it's time we went to bed'

Wife: 'You go if you want to dear. I must finish this before I turn out the sitting room tomorrow'

Husband: 'I think it is wonderful how you get everything done with me and the children to look after and no maid'

Wife: 'That's one of the nicest things you've said to me for a long time dear, but you know I should never have had the strength if you hadn't made me take those Phyllosan tablets regularly'

Husband: 'Well the older you get, the harder you seem to have to work. So let's be thankful Phyllosan is there to help you. A woman's work is never done!'

What a love! Although the most popular drugs alongside Phyllosan, Librium, and Valium, turned out to be habit-forming, they were hailed as miracle drugs for the stresses of midlife and menopause. Quick to ensure their marketplace lasted, drug companies recognized that post-menopause could be defined as a chronic state of depression, and, of course, lifelong medical management.

Feminist movement from the 1970s

By the end of the 1970s, women's independence had gathered momentum and half of all women were working (although at much lower wages than men). For the first time in history women could imagine that if they left home – or were cast out – they would survive and even (whisper it) thrive. Yet centuries of medicalizing older women's reproductive bodies were not going to loosen their grip that easily! The stereotypes of the older woman continued to flourish. Two US organizational scholars, Laurie Rudman and Peter Glick, started to study the impact of gender stereotypes and suggested that the historical stereotype of the older woman as lacking in youthful energy 'acted like an invisible force field or a cultural virus, pressuring people to act in ways that perpetuate the disease model. The result is a slow pace of change.'[21]

Fast forward to the 21st century and the reproductive body still remains a problem. Even when women are no longer fertile, their 'unreliable' bodies are presented in contrast to the stable, bounded, male 'norm'. My amazing (and very patient!) PhD supervisor Professor Caroline Gatrell has consistently challenged negative workplace beliefs about pregnant women and menopausal women being unstable and unable to control themselves. As she says,

> while men may be thought of as rational thinkers, inhabiting bodies that are imagined to be robust and unequivocal, the reverse is true for women. At work, rather than invoking visions of physical strength and sharp cognition (a warrior profile), female bodies are defined through their reproductive properties and women are treated as fragile and unstable – a problem for women seeking career advancement.[22]

She is very clear that the female body, whether pregnant, not pregnant, or menopausal, is still regarded as deficient and associated with illness, leading to negative evaluations of women's all-round functioning and intellect.

To the present day: female leadership

In every gender report, we lament the glacial pace of change for gender equality across the world. What this chapter shows is that, with a long historical shadow, women remain bounded to the association with intuitive, rather than reasoned action. Centuries of associating the female body with eroticism, frailty, passivity, and softness, and the male body with power, manliness, struggle, and dynamism, have enabled men to represent rationality and authority, with women representing the losing of control, or the losing of rationality. Cross-cultural studies reveal the pervasiveness and permanence of such character traits, indicating that people across the globe associate men with agency, power and dominance, and women with nurturance, succorance, and deference.[23] Across nations, men are still associated with power and status, and women with 'likeability' – in a nutshell, people like women but have greater respect for men.

With women's link to childrearing, people associate them with communal traits (e.g. helpful, nurturing, and kind), and men with more assertive, competitive, and aggressive traits, for their non-domestic work roles. This so-called 'social role theory'[24] also gives a great explanation for the slow pace of gender equality change. That is, the so-called 'proper places' for men and women, that support the ideals of a modern family system, also support an economic system, power structures, and social formation. And guess what, for older women comes the 'Grandmother Hypothesis'[25] – that is, the theory that suggests older women are only thriving and vigorous post-menopause in order to look after their grandchildren. Notice it's called the Grand*mother* theory, not parent or father!

So, as history replays itself, organizations still persist with the wearisome association of female leaders with 'soft' traits – also known as 'low status' traits – enabling men to claim the 'high status' traits. Reports abound that suggest a female leadership advantage here, with the demand in modern business for a less autocratic, more participative style of leadership.[26] The rise of so-called 'transformational leadership' or 'emotional leadership' has led some scholars to see a natural fit for women in such a leadership role. But if female leaders remain associated with sensitivity, modesty, and warmth, this 'niceness prescription' – also known as 'benevolent sexism' – handicaps women as they compete with men in the workplace.[27]

More worrying is how the Victorian script is being echoed by contemporary neurologists and psychologists who argue for the essential differences in the brain mapping of men and women. Professor Simon Baron-Cohen, Director of Psychology at the University of Cambridge, contends the female brain's propensity for understanding others' thoughts and feelings suits women for occupations that professionalize women's traditional caring roles, with the gender gap having neurological and hormonal roots.[28] Hardwired differently from men, psychologist Steven Pinker challenges the assumed desire of women for equality in the workplace, asserting their preference for family over career,[29] and Louann Brizendine claims in her book, *The Female Brain*, that the 'mommy brain' is far too overloaded for new ideas or career ambitions.[30]

Interestingly, this continuation of masculine and feminine leadership traits comes at a time when research is demonstrating either little difference between male/female perceived leadership effectiveness, or even that female leaders are more effective. And evidence keeps pouring in that companies with more female leaders outperform those dominated by men.[31] To mark International Women's Day in the UK, in 2022, data from the House of Commons library was collated, showing that companies in the top quartile for gender diversity on executive teams were 25% more likely to have above-average profitability than companies in the bottom quartile. Equally, companies with more than 30% female executives were more likely to outperform companies with fewer women at the top.

Given these optimistic statistics about the impact of female executives on company performance and productivity, you would think organizations would be fighting among themselves to retain their senior, middle-aged women, or at least we would witness a visible outcry about their levels of attrition. The silence with which this is greeted tells you everything you need to know about power. That is, male power has been hard fought for across the centuries and will not be easily relinquished. With every century, male scientists have applied themselves to medicalize the reproductive, and non-reproductive, body, enabling the identification of female executives with vulnerability, and placing women squarely back in the patriarchy. When so-called 'soft' leadership skills are labelled as 'feminine', it renders female executives in a deferential position. The legacy of centuries of 'making women sick' has erected powerful but subtle, invisible barriers for middle-aged women to progress, that arise from cultural assumptions, organizational structures and patterns of interaction that benefit men, whilst putting women at a disadvantage. Or as feminist campaigner Caroline Criado-Perez has asserted: 'No one seems to notice that women are routinely silenced. It's a very dishonest engagement.'[32]

PART 2

COLLISION

All beginnings are delightful. The threshold is the place to pause.

(Goethe)

CHAPTER 4

THE FRAGILE THRESHOLD OF MIDLIFE

Eventually we realize that not knowing what to do is just as real and just as useful as knowing what to do. Not knowing stops us from taking false directions. Not knowing what to do, we start to pay real attention. Just as people lost in the wilderness, on a cliff face or in a blizzard pay attention with a kind of acuity that they would not have if they thought they knew where they were. Why? Because for those who are really lost, their life depends on paying real attention. If you think you know where you are, you stop looking.

(David Whyte, *The Three Marriages: Reimagining Work, Self and Relationship*)[1]

Midlife is a transitional age. And it's messy and complicated, often leaving midlife women gasping for breath, for a break, a pause. Sometimes, by disconnecting each midlife event (think menopause, parental care, or children leaving home), it's easy to forget the sum of the whole. No wonder women walk away from their beautiful full-time careers, as they experience juggling like never before, emotional wrangling, or simply, as Lori said, 'a tsunami of stuff'.

And so the purpose of Part 2 is to highlight some of the unique circumstances that can fell a woman's career – often at its height. Whilst I'll examine each in turn in subsequent chapters, think menopause, caring, and existential angst, our starting point is exploring what happens when these events collide.

My study showed that midlife felt like a collision for the participants. I don't know why this surprised me, as in the five years from start to completion of the research, I experienced most aspects of life related by participants. After a difficult peri-menopause, I have in the last two years experienced some of the post-menopausal zest described to me by participants. Interestingly, as some participants related their hot flushes in rich detail, I experienced them again in the moment. That's empathy! Both my children started and graduated from university, leaving home for good to set up their respective lives elsewhere, with all the concurrent emotions of pride, concern, loss, and joy. In this time period, my father died of dementia and alcoholism, my mother-in-law descended for years into Alzheimer's, and my father-in-law more recently suffered delirium, a stroke, and a broken hip. With our siblings, my partner and I have shared their care, travelling the country to answer urgent caring calls.

My 94-year-old mother remains a vibrant source of joy and we share a desire to make the most of our remaining time, travelling together. (As she has recently published her first children's stories, she became a writing 'study buddy', and we stole away to Devon twice a year to write for four-day stretches.) My partner and I moved house and our thriving business hit a bumpy patch when I took time off for health reasons, and then it ground to a halt in the pandemic (like so many people, it climbed back out in a different shape and form than before).

At a deeper autobiographical level, it became apparent over the course of five years that 'life was imitating art' with many of the research questions reflecting my own personal age and stage of life as I grappled with the midlife questions of middle-aged identity, caring challenges, and ambition. There were countless times I got lost (commonly during data analysis!), stumbling to find my way back, with my supervisor providing a gentle, guiding hand.

The midlife 'smash up'

I still remember interviewing Lori. Quietly spoken, a senior talent director of a global firm, Lori heard about this project and requested to be part of it. Lori is 50, has twin 16-year-old daughters, is the main earner for the household and, up until recently, worked full-time. In the space of a year, her life changed, with a collision of events encompassing the menopause, her mum, and one of her daughters.

> *It wasn't so much the hot flushes or night sweats; the biggest issue was sleep. I couldn't sleep, I became desperate. My GP was fabulous, a real expert on women's health and after much deliberation, I started on HRT. But that was just one of the reasons I stepped back. My mum is 80, she's got heart disease and a whole plethora of other health-related issues. She took a big nose dive last year and to be frank, I just don't know how much longer I have with her, and I just decided I wanted to be around, I want to be there for her. But the third trigger is that one of my daughters is sadly battling anorexia. It's hard Lucy, really, really hard.*

Over the course of my time with Lori, what was clear was the lack of control that made this so hard. At no point in her life had she felt so vulnerable or helpless:

> *With a mental illness like anorexia, I'm just not really prepared for it as a parent. It's the hardest thing I've had to do, and still do, as a parent because to see your child in that kind of pain and angst it just rips your heart open, it really does and there is no simple solution. There is no, now I go and do this (snap) and then I do that (snap) and it gets fixed. It just doesn't work like that. Unfortunately,*

with mental illness there's no kind of end game. It's not something we can control at all. Being a business woman, you're used to being able to control things, fix things, sort things and we can't you know, I'm not able to do that.

It looked as if Lori would have to leave her job. That she didn't is a story for the end of the chapter.

Loss and letting go

It helps to see midlife as a transition, or a threshold. The need to 'let go' of one phase of your life before embracing the next. Metaphorically, thresholds are connected with the breaking point of a life, the moment of crisis, the decision that changes a life – or the indecisiveness that fails to change a life, the fear to step over the threshold. Over the course of exploring the lives of middle-aged women, I realized that there is a fragility in the midlife transition that either prevents growth and change or, at its best, is the natural precursor to revolution and transformation. In every single interview, the subject of 'loss', in one form or another, was discussed, together with the impact of this on the respondent's decisions about work and their relationship with their current employer. Discussions included the loss (or potential loss) of parents and friends, the departure of children, the loss of a career. The perceived loss of sexuality or fertility was considered along with the sense of loss of beauty, youth, and fitness, and often of identity. Emotions were high, with fear, guilt, exhaustion, uneasiness, and disappointment existing alongside those of joy, relief, liberation, astonishment, and abundance.

Not only this, but my study showed me that there was a different kind of 'letting go' happening: the letting go of old jobs or ways of working. Two-thirds of respondents were, at the time of interviewing, in the midst of career changes. This is, quite frankly, astonishing! In contrast to the literature suggesting the trajectory for professionals at middle age is one of decline and out, the range of career movement was heading in all directions. There were as many women in the process of stepping up within their organizations, as there were moving to self-employment; with further transitions including starting a job-sharing role; facing retirement; or embarking on student life. Of those who were not currently in the midst of flux, the desire (or intent) to change in the near future was much discussed – with intended moves including the prospect of future challenging roles within and outside of their organizations, or retirement.

For some of the women I talked to, the threshold is hopeful, a stepping up, 'a beautiful adventure'. For others, it is confusing, 'a crazy, challenging age', a stage where they need support to understand and cross the threshold. Or support to stay in their roles. But what we do know is that this state of midlife transition is disorientating. William Bridges is my go-to author on managing transitions.[2] A therapist in the 1970s, he published the famous book *Transitions: Making Sense of Life's Changes*, and reinvented himself in the 1990s with a swift nod to the business marketplace, with his book *Managing Transitions*. I'm a sucker for simple and profound models, and Bridges does exactly this. In a nutshell, his model shows the importance of 'letting go' before embracing new beginnings, lest we get stuck in the 'muggy middle'. What he is saying is that change itself is just a process, an event. But a transition is psychological. That is, in order to navigate any change, or incorporate it into our lives, we have to ensure we have embraced it mentally and emotionally, worked it through – head and heart.

Loss itself, whether of perceived beauty, youth, sexuality, or visibility, does not necessarily have a direct impact on career decisions. But at midlife, there is a breadth and depth of potential loss that gives rise to a vulnerability or an insecurity. And whilst loss enables us to regain a sense of the world, and can nourish us, it can also be threatening and close you down to future opportunities. This fragile time sees an increase in the thresholds women are asked to straddle. Feminist leadership scholars, Professors Sharon Mavin and Gina Grandy note how women traverse the 'complex, ambiguous and precarious in-betweens of masculinity/ femininity, revealing/hiding one's body, conservative/ fashionable dress, social conformity/individual creativity and sexuality/asexuality'.[3] In a similar way, women within this data set negotiate the transition between ageing/ youth, sexual/de-sexualized body, disease/liberation with menopause, full-time parent/part-time parent. These fragile thresholds, the balance between losing or gaining control, can be very tenuous at this challenging age. Invisible to research, to organizational literature or even casual conversations, midlife women navigate this universe of seesaws, mingled identity, fears, and struggles, often with a fixed 'I'm fine' smile on their face.

Constrained choices

In the limited research on midlife women that explores why they exit from corporate life to self-employment, or 'opt out' of organizations, the transition is described as a 'constrained choice'.[4] That is, the extraordinary flux of changing circumstances I mentioned earlier is not always the woman's choice – but one forced upon them. And it's not just women exiting the company – sometimes the 'stepping up' or remaining at work is also a constrained choice. And that's because midlife is shown to be a time during which there are significant increases in the *proportion* of stressors. It's called 'role overload'[5] and wow, do I recognize that term! Professional women are coping with a complex collision of care (children, siblings, partners, and parents), together with financial, work and health issues (menopause or otherwise). All of which have physical, mental, and emotional manifestations.

Of all my interviewees, Chris struck me as the woman most constrained by circumstance with a collision of divorce, redundancy, financial and family issues. Divorced two years ago, coping with a difficult relationship with her ex-husband and two children, she lost her job aged 55, due to a company merger. She describes this as a 'huge, huge shock', suffering grief from being separated from the people she called her 'work family'. She has a new job she loves, but, being on probation, she must work full-time (or 24/7 as she suggests) whilst also managing the complex needs of her father in a care home, without the support of her siblings. The inability to control events is proving demanding:

> *I feel more pressured now than I probably did when I had the kids at home when I was 30 because a lot of the stuff I can't fix, but it's exhausting, it's absolutely exhausting. I'd love to say, 'well it all doesn't matter, and I'm kicking back, and they can fire me if they want, and fuck the lot of them and I'm just going to go around the world for a year'. But it doesn't feel like that. It feels worse. I've now got a mortgage and the kids need money. And I'm fine now but I have a lot of anxiety, I've got no safety nets in my life, there is no back up. There is no back up.*

For many women, though, work is the only place that offers control, particularly in a life where other plans and dreams have been abandoned. In 1997 sociologist Arlie Hochschild wrote a book called *The Time Bind: When Work Becomes Home and Home Becomes Work.*[6] She concluded that the roles of home and work had reversed: work had become more attractive, offering a sense of belonging, while home had grown more stressful, becoming a dreaded place with too many demands. Women recognized this, and the book became an instant, and sustained, bestseller.

Work is both a refuge and a necessity for Robin, 62, whose husband suffered chemical poisoning early in their marriage and ongoing heart problems as a result. Robin is a board director for a UK charity. As well as working full-time, she cares for her husband, and is managing their limited funds, as the couple spent their savings pursuing (and losing) a legal case against her husband's ex-employers. Robin's constrained choice is the abandonment of her retirement plans:

> So we've kind of got to a place where we've stopped making plans. It was just, let's get through this. Because it just got dark, too painful. We are still in the same house we moved into when we first got together which wasn't our plan, so we sort of stopped thinking longer term.

Stepping into the threshold

This chapter presents one of the most startling conclusions from my study. That is, it is not necessarily the separate and unique events that happen to women in their middle years that cause them to exit their organization, but the collision. I'm not alone in reaching this conclusion. Eleanor Mills, founder and editor-in-chief of Noon, an online platform for women at midlife, led the UK's most in-depth study of ABC1 women aged 45–60 undertaken in Britain (2,000 women). She discovered that half of the women in their study had experienced five or more traumatic events by midlife, including menopause, death, anxiety, or divorce.[7] It's the maelstrom of these events that can be overwhelming. And what is more tragic for the woman, and the organization that loses her talent, is that commonly the events that make up this collision are temporary. Peri-menopause passes, parents leave this earth, children mature, and women learn to address their new transitions in novel ways.

For those women I interviewed who had left their roles early, there was a wistfulness for what has gone before and is lost forever. Donna, 55, so dynamic when talking about her middle years and her non-executive roles, describes her regret at giving up her full-time job of CEO to manage her life: 'I sort of regret giving up because I could have, I think I could have done greater things in my career.' Adriana, 55, was an interesting interviewee as she had just resigned that week from her role as a senior manager within the FMCG sector. It was a role she loved, but a complex takeover meant a shift in team, role, salary, benefits, and future growth. She spent much of the interview describing her joy of early retirement, yet hesitantly ventured at the end:

> At the time when I was most stressed, if they had intervened then with some real help I probably wouldn't have got to the stage where I was like, 'yeah right, this is not worth it'. I just needed help, and (if it was given) I would have not turned away, resigned, and seen it as done.

And back to Lori:

Lori decided she had to leave her job, but one extraordinary circumstance changed this. Picture this: Lori takes the elevator down to the coffee shop to write her resignation letter. In the lift she gets talking to her colleague, a peer in the human resources directorate, who had reluctantly resigned that morning. With three children under 12, and a dying father, her colleague had decided she couldn't manage anymore. Together, over coffee, they craft a job share, which is accepted for one post and a full-time new hire agreed for the other.

Clearly, Lori is in a fortunate position job-wise. She and her colleague knew their way around the HR system, they shared a (male) boss, they both had a solid reputation, and understood the value they brought to the firm. It was the first job share ever offered globally and, hopefully, not the last. But this doesn't take away from the fact that, were it not for this chance meeting, two valuable middle-aged women would have been lost to this organization. And Lori is anything but naïve about the potential for a different ending:

> *Had I just said, please can I step down to three days a week, without a resolution for how my full-time job would get done, he'd have said, I'd love to help but sorry, it's a full-time job. I served him up an answer on a plate, and it was in his best interests to agree.*

Lori's story begs a question, why aren't companies creating a structure so that women are not dependent on chance meetings to remain in their roles? And why is it so seemingly impossible for flexibility at a senior level? At the start of the book I suggested there are three ways in which midlife women are discriminated against in the workplace: they're not young, not male, and not full-time. Women described the impossibility of going part-time in a more senior role, as Claire wryly stated, 'I inched my days from 3, to 3½, from 4 to 4½ to well, fuck it, I might as well be full time'. The practical implications of midlife collisions can render this impossible, hence, one by one, your midlife talent drains away.

CHAPTER 5

MENOPAUSE: FACTS AND FRICTIONS

As someone who has dedicated the last six years of her career to breaking workplace menopause taboos, I keep coming back to the importance of education to bust myths. For most people, menopause is a normal and natural process and a phase in their reproductive life course that doesn't go on forever and needn't be an off-limits topic. Everyone ought to know what this thing is, who it affects and how diverse an experience it can be. The more we keep this conversation going and amplify it, the more we'll understand menopause and the better we'll be able to support those who struggle through the experience. The time has more than come.

(Jo Brewis, Professor of People and Organisations, Open University)[1]

Five years ago I beat a path to the door of a UK literature festival to see two renowned journalists talking about their new books on midlife and menopause to a sold-out public platform of 1,200 women. I was excited – only five years ago the topics you're reading about here were still relatively taboo. Yet in the following hour, every part of the middle-aged female body was available for exhaustive negative dissection. In case the audience were not aware, the authors assured everyone that at midlife the following will happen: your hair thins; your beard starts; your eyelids droop (so don't bother with make-up); knees sag; give up jogging – you're too fat, and don't bother dressing up, no one is going to notice you. Sex was described as 'grotesque and impossible' and the menopause 'a chamber of horrors'. A message of acceptance was suggested as being the sole positive route forwards, with women advised to accept that their sex life 'will be going downhill and will stop very soon'. Further advice included to acknowledge their invisibility as their looks had already gone (and it will get worse), and to recognize the menopause will 'ruin your life', with recovery unlikely.

Unfortunately this is not an unusual message. Shrouded in 'ha-ha, we'll all sink together' humour, menopause is just one of the misunderstood midlife collisions that causes many women confusion, awkwardness, and shame. It might not be the exact reason why women are leaving your workplace, but it is likely to be one of the triggers. To some extent the silence that has enveloped the menopause discussion is being currently addressed in the UK. Menopause is having its moment thanks to celebrities like Davina McCall and Penny Lancaster, who by working together with campaigners and MPs, including the Rt Hon Caroline Nokes and Carolyn Harris, have forced menopause into the open, broken barriers and laws, enabling taboo words like 'vaginal atrophy' and 'night sweats' to come out from behind the sniggering back hand. But there is some way to go. In 2023, the UK government resisted calls to make menopause a 'protected characteristic', rejecting the proposal for a pilot scheme on menopause leave as 'unnecessary'.[2] This is despite the fact that studies and statistics abound of the cost to women (and to business) that arises from ignoring this natural phase of an older woman's life,[3] including:

- In a robust UK study, half of women going through the menopause reported difficulty coping with symptoms at work; yet two-thirds said they would not dream of disclosing their menopausal status to their bosses, male or female.

- One in ten women in the UK leave the workplace due to menopausal symptoms.
- A poll of 1,009 women aged 50 to 60 carried out for Radio 4's *Woman's Hour* in 2018 found that nearly half of respondents said the menopause had affected their mental health, while a quarter said it made them want to stay at home. Seventy per cent of women did not make their employer aware they were experiencing symptoms, and a third had not visited their GP, remaining silent.
- Women who experience the most distress report as being the least likely to disclose this due to embarrassment or fear of being stereotyped. Specific reasons for non-disclosure include:
  - Not wanting their line manager to think their performance had been or could be affected
  - Finding disclosure embarrassing
  - Having a male or younger manager
  - Concerns about confidentiality
  - Fears of being labelled 'hysterical', 'histrionic', or 'menopausal-ish'
- According to one extensive cross-industry report, negative reactions to the women in transition are especially likely in male-dominated occupations like the police service or the army.
- Yet, in an NUT survey (National Union of Teachers, UK, 2014), a female-dominated profession, only 18% of respondents said there was a climate of openness, with reports of bullying, mocking, teasing, and disparagement.
- In the 2022 UK government survey, Women in the Workplace, witnesses told the committee that menopause-related discrimination was widespread and shocking, with women forced to frame claims as sex, age, or even disability discrimination.

Defining the menopause

For a stage of a woman's life that should be easy to understand, to recognize and to treat, it is both extraordinary and frustrating how the menopause is swathed in mixed messages and polarized debates. Current debates on the menopause demonstrate a complex array of interested parties spanning physicians and pharmaceutical manufacturers, medical and non-medical researchers, feminist scholars, anthropologists, social scientists, industry bodies, celebrities, retail, the government, the media, and consumers – all with their individual case to argue, and some with money to make on the back of their argument. According to one recent report, the global menopause market represents a $600 billion (£450 bn) business opportunity.[4] It's the so-called 'menopause goldrush' and they want your money. Little wonder midlife women feel like the pivot of a weathervane, swinging in every opiniated direction depending on where the wind is blowing that week.

So what do scientists agree on? Well, this is limited to the definition of the menopause. That is, menopause occurs when a woman's periods stop and her ovaries cease producing significant amounts of the hormones oestrogen and progesterone. This can occur naturally, due to a diminishing number of eggs – usually between the ages of about 45 and 55 – or it can occur prematurely, if the ovaries are surgically removed, for example, or damaged by treatments such as chemotherapy or radiotherapy. According to the World Health Organization, a woman is assumed to be post-menopausal one year after her last period.[5]

Oestrogen affects the body in many ways – from brain function to bone density, skin elasticity, vaginal lubrication, and the distribution of fat, so losing it causes organs and tissues to behave differently. However, this transition does not occur overnight. Peri-menopause (or menopause transition) refers to the time leading up to a woman's last menstrual period. Reporting in *The Guardian* in 2022, Dr Paula Briggs, a consultant in sexual and reproductive health at Liverpool Women's NHS Foundation Trust, and chair-elect of the British Menopause Society, suggests,

> *during that time (perimenopause), women's hormones are very variable. These fluctuating hormone levels underpin some of the symptoms women experience, such as heavy or irregular periods, heart palpitations or mood swings. As perimenopause progresses, women may experience other symptoms, such as hot flushes, night sweats, sleeplessness, skin irritation, anxiety, or a reduced interest in sex. You do get women who will go through that transition with absolutely no symptoms whatsoever, but very few women will get away without anything at all.*[6]

For centuries women suffered in silence. Even today, women are viewed as falling into one of two camps: those who view menopause as a disease, a hormone deficiency, or disability, to be treated with HRT (hormone replacement therapy) to alleviate symptoms; and those who see menopause as a natural phase of life to be celebrated, not medicalized, treated, or pathologized. It's unfortunate these debates can get pretty ugly, particularly as the pendulum keeps swinging. Evidence is mounting that some of the fears of HRT may have been overblown and although it is not risk-free, women should be allowed to take it for life. Dr Louise Newson is one of strongest proponents of HRT in the UK. She leads a private menopause clinic, and also offers a fabulous (free) 'balance' menopause app. She says, 'menopause is a hormone deficiency, but people have been scared away from their own hormones because of poor data, and because of scaremongering in the media and medical press'.[7]

What worries me about polarized debates is they create more confusion for women, just at the point of needing good information from a trusted source, and preclude women from having a foot in both camps. Such arguments leave little space for nuance or for individual experience, with women in an uncertain position as to whether to fear or cheer the menopause.

The lived experience at work

Broadly, research agrees that between 10 and 20% of women will experience severe menopausal symptoms that will have a strong, negative impact on their life and at work, with a similar percentage experiencing limited or no symptoms.[8] This leaves roughly 60% of women in a 'muggy middle' of troublesome problems or in a position of uncertainty. In the UK government's 2022 'Menopause and the Workplace' report, many women spoke of a lack of awareness of understanding of menopause and feeling unprepared for the effect it would have on their lives. Dr Nighat Arif, a GP and specialist in women's health and family, described there being a 'misogyny within medicine when it comes to women's health'.[9]

And women in my study broadly echoed the research. Fifty per cent of women replied to questions regarding their menopausal experience with a variation on the answer of 'no idea' or 'not sure'. Their responses can be divided into two groups: those women who had a physical intervention causing uncertainty as to whether they were menopausal or not, and those who experienced no symptoms. Looking at the first group, the physical interventions included contraception (the pill, the Mirena coil, or depo injection); an elected endometrial ablation; early hysterectomy for fibroid treatment; side effects of chemotherapy outweighing menopausal symptoms; and IVF treatment causing a cessation of periods. In the second group, a further ten women experienced no symptoms and therefore assumed themselves to be post-menopausal.

Some women displayed an indifference to the menopause with no sense of reluctance, embarrassment, or fear. Nora stated, 'I didn't notice it all really', and Ana held menopause at arm's length, 'Well I've had absolutely nothing to do with it.' These discussions around the menopause were relatively short, commonly accompanied by an apology for not having much to say, or Ana's expression of guilt: 'I don't dare tell my girlfriends because some of them are having such rubbish times and I had absolutely nothing.'

Whilst there's an interesting reflection here about whether women feel the need to be silent if their experience of menopause is relatively non-existent, all the women I interviewed agreed that, despite recent publicity, there still remained a virtual silence in the workplace around this topic, and that the silence had negative consequences. For every woman who has an 'OK' experience, there is another for whom it is difficult.

Jude's rich description of her current problematic peri-menopause is useful for understanding the practical difficulties of menopausal symptoms in the workplace:

I think it feels tough sometimes because I'm sweating, hot, in pain and uncomfortable. I look in the mirror and feel awful some days. For example, this week I had the board meeting on Tuesday. So, the board is starting at lunchtime and I am extra hot, extra sweaty, extra curly hair, extra make-up round my chin rather than on my face, and I'm thinking, I've got to stand and present. So, my routine was on Tuesday morning, get in early, have a change of clothing with me as well, in the same colour, take all my make-up, all my stuff and before I go in at 12, at 11 I'm in the toilets sorting myself out. Then

I'm boiling sorting myself out and so my hair is already curling as I'm straightening, then you feel conscious of it cos you're so hot and warm and you want to make a good impression. Plus remembering what I'm going to be saying for the day. I don't think anyone realizes what that feels like unless you have to sit there and do it. And then you do the session and feel brilliant and walking to the toilet and thinking I'm going to burst into tears and just like, where did that come from? That makes you think, can I, will I, can I continue and control it enough in a normal conversation?

Unsurprisingly, being the sole woman on the board, Jude recognized that an open discussion on the menopause at work could be construed as 'having a serious illness' and as seeming less than competent. Yet, the women interviewed believed that an open dialogue in the workplace on the menopause could only be a positive alternative to silence. Kristin, previously HR director of a sizeable media company and an advocate for compassion at work, is explicit on the needs of the organization to bring the menopause conversation alive in the workplace:

I think for me a big thing is around the physical changes and, linked into that, the emotional changes of the menopause that we don't pay any attention to in the workplace. For example, the embarrassment of hot flushes. I've been in meetings where people have had hot flushes and that whole sense of how people around the room respond to that, how they feel about that happening. I just don't think we talk about it enough or understand it as a phase. We need to make much clearer, better provision for this.

What these women are expressing is the desire for a normal-ization of the menopause discussion. Not a normalization of women's pain, or the stoic response to 'live with it', but a conversation that recognizes individual experience, laced with compassion. For example, Kathleen, 55, discussed one instance of post-menopausal bleeding which happened suddenly in the office some 14 months after her last period, which she found shocking, embarrassing and 'hideous, just hideous'. For her, a 'normal' discussion is:

> *It's just trying to get it across that it's a perfectly natural thing that happens. Recognize that it's okay to talk about it and perhaps even having an acknowledgement that you might have to go home and that's okay. I mean for me that day I just wanted to go home. I felt dirty, I felt really uncomfortable, embarrassed. It would be helpful just to know there is someone that you can go and talk to.*

The common refrain for so many women in transition is, 'I just didn't feel like me'. These are Esme's words, who was shocked at her change from being a high-achieving senior manager in the tech industry, to feeling under-confident, hot, sweaty, embarrassed, and a sense of being unable to function at her best at work. Lack of sleep and anxiety meant that Esme decided to leave her company. She had no other plan, she says, 'other than to stop pretending I could perform at the desired level'. But Esme is one of the fortunate women who sought internal help from HR, and got it. A series of open and honest conversations between Esme, HR and her manager led to an individualized flexible working policy that enabled her to stay in her role, and she describes HRT as 'saving her life'. Even better, Esme brought in workplace menopause experts and now co-facilitates menopause masterclasses for people in her company, so that women can share their experience; men understand what is going on with their partners and their reports; and younger women join the conversation. As she states,

> *what's important here is we talk about menopause openly, it's understood there is no 'one size fits all', and women*

know what's likely to come and can make informed decisions about how they want to manage that part of their life.

The positive menopause

There is also solid research that suggests menopause can be a positive, liberating event. I don't mean in a Pollyanna, let's wave our incense sticks around, kind of way. I mean, can the menopause actually provide women with a physical and mental benefit? Yes, it seems so, and I'm curious if reporting is so quiet about this as it might disavow those who are suffering. Or sometimes only shocking, negative stories sell. This came into sharp focus for me in January 2018 when I was asked by BBC Radio Sheffield to talk about the menopause on their live link-up with *Woman's Hour.* I noted in my journal,

> *I've just had my pre-interview and discussed how women want to break the silence, but equally want the menopause discussion normalized, not pathologized. The interviewer doesn't want this angle and wants to highlight only those having a hard time. I said this did happen but was only some of the story, with other women experiencing benefit, and have since been 'relegated' to the tea-time show.*

Yet within my study at least four women wanted to talk about their positive menopause. Meg, 57, stated how much more 'emotionally stable' and 'productive at work' she now felt without the upheaval of PMT (pre-menstrual tension), and Gail, 61, concurred:

> *I flew through my menopause in a way, but what I realized is that I wasn't feeling exhausted like I used to when I was having periods. There used to be times when I wanted to curl up and you know what it is but urgh, always on a major presentation day. And then I started to realize that*

I wasn't carrying tampaxes in pockets, I wasn't thinking about it, I was through it. I had hot sweats at night but thought I was worrying about the business. After a year or so, I realized I felt great. A real sense of freedom. My head was clear. Before menopause I'd have headaches, even migraines, or just not feel 100%. But now I have the reverse of brain fog. It was like a release.

Far from losing control of the body, Eve, 54, whom you met in the Introduction, talked about the menopause giving her a sense of control:

I'm much more attentive to my body now. Not menstruating has made me feel more in control. So, my body just feels more contained, more my own, it feels I'm steadier now too as I haven't got those monthly rhythms in terms of my mental state. It feels like I'm much more in control of my body, my life, which feels good.

These positive findings are interesting because they're so different from those in the majority of studies. In contrast to negative accounts of the effects of physical and psychological transition symptoms on economic participation, the Social Issues Research Centre's UK survey (SIRC 2002) saw 50% of female respondents aged 50–64 saying their capacity to work and develop their careers had increased since they entered menopause transition.[10] Lotte Hvas, from the University of Copenhagen, led a rare study on the positive aspects of the menopause, with 70% of the 393 women questioned offering positive statements, including menopause as a period of well-being, relief at ending menstruation, and personal growth.[11]

Shifting the organizational culture

What this means is that to shift the organizational culture in the workplace will take more than a 'one size fits all' approach. Moreover, rather than just examining menopause from a positive/negative aspect, some scientists describe it as a 'bio-psycho-social-cultural' phenomenon.[12] That is, as explained in the previous chapter, menopause occurs precisely at the time that other midlife changes or difficulties are being experienced – it's one of the midlife collisions. Far from being an isolated event, menopausal symptoms occur within the wider psychological and social context of a woman's life, including her lifestyle, her attitude to ageing and, importantly, the cultural space surrounding the role and status of older women in that society, community – or indeed in her workplace. This is a life stage which is complicated by more than just a change in reproductive capacity. Juliet's story is useful here as she finds herself aged 55 wrestling with biological, social, and psychological transitions. Juliet is a GP, and she and her wife decided in their early 50s to adopt two young siblings with special needs. As her partner, a lawyer, has given up work to look after the children, Juliet has gone back to working full-time in order to provide the family with financial stability. As both her parents are ill and disabled, not only does Juliet have little time to visit them but there is limited childcare support. Fitness is important to her mental well-being and a critical part of her positive identity, but with time squeezed and energy depleted, she states: 'I just feel like I am the older lady, so I'm doing my treadmill, but you know I can't kick ass, I think that is a real loss'. Juliet associates her perceived physical weakness with the menopause:

> I think I have felt much physically weaker, losing muscle mass, and waking up with hot flushes. It's difficult to know whether I feel more emotional because I'm more tired with the kids, or moods due to the life changes or the actual menopause. It's chicken and egg. I'm blaming the menopause.

Some workplace menopause solutions can be clumsy at best or downright offensive at worst. In the clumsy category come workplace posters displaying definitive negative menopause symptoms. Seen in one of my clients offices was this poster:

> *Menopause will cause depression! Insomnia! Weight gain! Irritability!*

Watch out for the menopausal woman. Or in the negative category, coming in at number one is the organization which offered badges to all female employees over 50, bearing the phrase 'I'm hot!' Oh dear. Little surprise that women I interviewed felt disempowered and disenchanted, or as Kathleen said: 'I don't want to be seen as a walking hot flush'.

So what does work? Women can and are doing things for themselves. This includes monitoring their bleeding patterns; reconsidering their diet and exercise plans; taking HRT and/or embracing talking therapy; stashing fresh supplies of sanitary protection in several places and wearing dark garments. (A wool duvet was my sanity.) But these frame the menopause transition as an individual problem, rather than something which can be made more difficult by workplace conditions and others' behaviour, so what we are clearly seeing is that organizations need to step up. What can they do?

First, there are straightforward hygiene factors that can be addressed. The evidence base suggests menopause symptoms can become more troublesome due to inadequate ventilation, high temperatures, humidity, and dryness – all of which increase hot flushes. Lack of access to appropriate toilet facilities, cold drinking water, or quiet rest areas can make the experience of heavy or irregular periods difficult. Confined work spaces or crowding can make the experience of hot flushes worse, as do unsuitable uniforms or heavy uncomfortable workwear.[13]

Second is the need to change attitudes and the workplace culture.[14] How do you do this? It's about developing a culture that embraces diversity in all its forms, and that includes an understanding of menopause with solid advice and support. It's about ensuring that the menopause conversation is not hidden and silent – it is de-stigmatized. As we saw above, both Jude and Kathleen would have valued someone to talk to and a place to share experience. Esme's example is a good demonstration of leading change through shifting workplace attitude.

So bring menopause into the open: hold talks, set up workplace menopause cafés, have mentors, and display an open menopause policy at work. Make it a policy topic: pregnancy and returning to work after maternity leave are commonplace topics in HR policy and equality legislation. The same is not true of the menopause. Make managers aware: training for line managers is still scant, and in every conference, masterclass, or menopause webinar I've delivered or attended, 99% of attendees are female. What we need is for the discussion to be broadened to include more employees, younger women, and men, and menopause to be made a normal part of your equality, diversity, and inclusion strategy.

And in addressing this, companies need to be aware that midlife women have fought hard to get to the place they are in an organization. They face enough gendered ageism, and know they are meant to manage their appearance to present an 'unproblematic body' at work – and this knowledge should inform how it is approached. With the 'cultural grammar' surrounding the menopause being that of distress and difficulty, and menopausal women over the centuries described as increasingly frail, the transition is still something working women prefer to keep to themselves, largely out of fear of being seen as less competent. Or, as Sandra described in an open discussion of menopause at work – 'professional suicide'.

The workplace culture that is lived by midlife women will affect the way they talk about, define, treat, accept, or fight their menopausal physical, mental, and emotional changes. They have no desire for marginalization but do require a normalization of this life stage faced by half the world's population. Women are culturally astute and consciously work their bodies to support the ongoing need for authority and credibility – when they fear they can no longer do this, commonly, they exit the system.

CHAPTER 6

WHO CARES?

Women work incredibly hard to care for others. Not only is this work unpaid, but it's often not seen as real work at all. If we valued care work the same as other work, it would be worth nearly $11 trillion US dollars a year. But its true value is much greater.

(www.oxfam.org)

When it comes to issues of care, emotions are heightened and heartfelt. As I interviewed Melissa, she wept describing the trauma of placing her mother in a care home.

I seemed to cope quite well up until one night she rang and was screaming down the phone, 'I hate it, I hate it, I hate it' and she just screamed and let this horrible scream out that I'd never heard before. I came off the phone and I was just traumatized, so it really affected me from then on, so I kind of coped for about six months and then it was all too much.

Melissa, 55, talked about her full-time role within content management with passion, and of begging them to let her go part-time, so she could care for her mum, her brother (who is bipolar and recently struggling) and keep her job. Their answer was that she was 'too valuable to lose any part of her'.

Trying to get to work on time, and get from work to where my mum lives, then get to the hospital, sort out mum, drive to my brother's house, get home again, I was exhausted, I wasn't sleeping at night, because, you know, there was too much going on, so I just couldn't cope with work anymore.

Unsurprisingly, Melissa resigned, setting up her own (now, very successful) software business three months after her mum died.

I recognize Melissa's emotional response. My mum and I had a telephone 'fine' code. As my dad's demented behaviour became increasingly unpredictable, mum would ring me, saying 'fine' between one to five times. One 'fine', and she's OK. Five 'fines' ('how are you mum today?' 'Fine fine fine fine fine, thanks darling'), and I'm in the car for another motorway dash, work on hold again.

Footloose and fancy free?

Whenever people talk about caring challenges facing women in the workplace, the discussion is commonly about younger women, with young children. And when the discussion turns to the older woman, there is an envious sigh of the supposed end of this challenge. Children have 'flown the nest' and the woman is footloose and fancy free! Research follows in a similar vein. When scholars discuss any kind of midlife 'resurgence', it is intimately linked with the notions of freedom and autonomy.[1] Government or academic reports, one after the other, repeat the same message, with statements such as 'the majority of those in their 50s no longer carry the burden of supporting children', 'living a life that is cash and time rich', whilst being 'free and autonomous'.[2]

I don't for a minute underestimate the difficulties younger women face with childcare, nor the independence enjoyed by some older women, but there are many other lived experiences going on here. The difference here lies in the stories of the multi-faceted caring responsibilities facing women at midlife, making a full-time presence in the workplace for some women seem impossible. If my data set is in any way representative of the caring responsibilities facing middle-aged women, the challenges are alarming.

- Almost half of the women had one or more parent with a form of dementia for whom they were actively involved with the caring
- One in ten women were caring for their seriously ill husband or a sibling
- One in five women were helping their older children cope with a mental illness
- One respondent was actively caring for her mum, her aunt, and her mother-in-law at the same time, whilst another was juggling seven grandchildren and a mother with locked-in syndrome

The impact of this is extraordinary: a third of respondents took a break, or stepped down, from their role, albeit temporarily, to manage these situations, with only one husband described as sharing the caring responsibility.

One-third took a break! Seriously, as my chapter heading asks, who cares?

Furthermore, the assumption that by midlife older mothers are 'empty nesters' appears to be far from reality. Half of my respondents still had dependent children living at home, with eight of the women interviewed still having two or more dependent children at home. Take Cyn, 46, a full-time nurse, with five dependent children, the youngest of whom is 6 years old. Full of humour and vivacity, Cyn still describes her life as 'physically and mentally exhausting' as she works 14-hour shifts so as to have a day off in the week to make childcare easier. Juliet, a full-time GP, also has two young children (aged 6 and 7), whom she and her partner adopted in their early 50s. In a similar way to any parent with young children, Juliet describes feeling equally tired and far too exhausted to discuss how she feels at midlife:

> *I think my life has been so overwhelmingly ruled by having the kids that actually everything else has gone by the by. I feel exhausted, so I'm not sure I've had much time to think how I feel (about midlife).*

The changing face of the family structure

The findings should not be a surprise as they reflect a number of societal demographic trends.[3] As we've seen, middle-aged people tend to have parents who are alive, with fewer siblings to share the caregiving. Adult children are likely to live further away from their parents, making the caregiving more complicated and disruptive. Women are having children at later stages, so their parents are older whilst their children still young. Support for children might last longer than that of their parents' generation, often reaching into their early and mid-20s as they acquire further learning or struggle to get on the property ladder. Alongside this, not only has the time we spend being married shrunk, but also fewer adults remarry, leading to a higher proportion living in single person households. Families continue to become more 'vertical' (i.e. more typically comprised of persons from three or more generations) and less 'horizontal' (i.e. fewer from the same generation), giving rise to more interdependency across the generations.[4]

Let's dig deeper into the changing face of the family in the 21st century, and particularly the trend for older motherhood.[5] Whilst parents are the group most often cared for by older women, children under 18 years are the next biggest age group, contradicting a widespread age assumption or 'norm' that women (or indeed, parents) over 50 are 'child-free'. In the latest reports available from the Office for

National Statistics, the age of mothers giving birth has risen steadily each year, and over half (51%) of all live births are now to mothers aged over 30, 22% being over 35, with 5% over 40 years.[6] For the first time since records began, more women over 40 are becoming pregnant than girls under 17. In the US, the widespread study of midlife adults, MIDUS, revealed that, of the 7,000 midlife adults studied aged 40–59, 38.8% had children under 18 years, with only 7.4% of women and 9.6% of men from these birth cohorts not having any children.[7] Recent 'YouGov' polling in the UK agrees, finding that more than one-third of parents aged between 45 and 54 have school-age children. Indeed, the last 10 years have seen an increase in fertility rates for women older than 35 in the UK, with the highest percentage increase occurring in women aged 40 and over. The number of births to women aged 40 or more in England and Wales trebled from 1989 to 2009, and this trend to older motherhood is in evidence in almost all developed countries.[8]

And let's include those women who do not have children: 18% of women who reached the age of 45 years in 2017 in the UK ended their childbearing years without children, compared with just 10% of women born in 1945.[9] Reasons offered for this statistical trend are: a decline in the proportion of women married; changes in the perceived costs and benefits of childrearing versus work and leisure activities; greater social acceptability of a child-free lifestyle; and the postponement of decisions as to whether to have children until it may be biologically too late.[10]

And what is the result of this? What my statistics show is that later motherhood, encouraged by companies and denigrated by society at large, is the reality of a huge percentage of women's lives. Older motherhood and later reproduction are consistently stressed – as much in the academic literature as in the media – as a medical, social, and economic cost to society.[11] Older mothers have been portrayed as both 'feckless and selfish',[12] even when the organization they work for is pressing them to delay childbirth, with the much publicized 'benefit' offered by large corporates to their female employees, of egg freezing – or, as Yvonne Roberts writes in *The Observer*, 'motherhood to suit the marketplace'.[13] Damned if you do, damned if you don't!

This simplification of the experience of women at midlife renders the real experience of midlife women as unimportant and invisible – yet again enabling their disappearance from the workplace but ensuring the unpaid caring work – the 'shadow workforce' – continues. And the more worrying trend is that post-pandemic, this is only increasing.[14] Prior to the pandemic of 2020, women were more likely to work outside of the home. This all changed with the return to the home in 2020. Post pandemic, we are witnessing a 'sticky' return to the household for midlife women, who are juggling paid work and unpaid caring more than ever. That is, their hard-fought right to go out to work has, in some cases, been replaced by a dependency on them back in the home. Oh yes, it was great when you were around!

'Dependants this way, that way'

Nina, 54, whom you briefly met earlier, is a business leader in retail, and found herself at midlife with two teenage children still at home, a difficult menopausal experience, a full-time job, whilst also caring for her mother, aunt, and mother-in-law. This was a time in her life she described as 'just unbelievable, full on, disturbing and very, very hard. I think my life has been either working and studying, or working and children, or working and caring.' At this point in her career, she didn't pursue any step up, stating that 'she didn't feel it was an option… with all the responsibility'.

Ines, 59, a senior professional within the food industry, had her twins at 42 years of age after egg donation. Her mum is healthy but housebound and her sister, who lives near her mum, has learning difficulties. At 53, Ines took eight months off work to recover from Hodgkin's lymphoma cancer and care for her teenage daughter with mental health issues. On returning to work and still needing flexibility, she described 'seeing the writing on the wall' and took redundancy. In a similar vein to Lori (whom you met in Chapter 4), Ines spoke with great love for her 15-year-old daughter who was struggling.

> I have to be available, she's 15. Everything you see about teenage mental health just sort of landed on her, and she got very anxious and very depressed. You are so powerless as a mum, but you have to be there.

Ines is working a few part-time jobs at the moment, and sounds resigned:

> I don't know, I am... I feel underutilized but it's like, of the available options at the moment, I am better to be underutilized. Better to be underutilized and available (to my daughter).

And what of the future, Ines?

> I suppose I wonder what could happen in two years' time when my daughter's finished school and hopefully off on her life. I think that's interesting. I definitely want to do more. I don't want to wind down, but I know that the world will be different in two years' time. But I actually find it quite hard to imagine a world when I don't have dependants this way or that way, or I don't have so many caring commitments and the world is changing so quickly I don't know what the next thing might be in two or three years' time.

The rising number of adults with dementia is increasingly documented, and, more slowly, so is the issue of adolescents with mental health challenges. For example, the World Health Organization reported in 2021 that, globally, one in seven 10–19-year-olds experiences a mental disorder, with depression, anxiety and behavioural disorders among the leading causes of illness.[15] Multiple factors are offered as reasons for this rise, including the relationship with parents and peers, exposure to adversity (e.g. the pandemic), pressure to conform with peers, and the exploration of identity. Media influence can exacerbate the disparity between an adolescent's lived reality and their perceptions or aspirations for the future.

What is left undocumented is the impact on parents for their care. There are few statistics that bear out the extent of this problem, so I can only rely on my own data, and anecdotal stories of friends and colleagues.

The hypocrisy economy

What I do know is that society at large is turning a very convenient blind eye to the extent of the problem of caring, and how this is ramped up for the midlife woman. This unpaid care work is variously called the *care economy*, the *core economy* and the *reproductive economy*. I like to call it the *hypocrisy economy*, that is, when people talk about empowering women, because they now also work outside the home in the paid economy, in addition to taking care of their children, parents and home, without any systemic attempt to encourage men to take more responsibility.

I'm not alone in believing that at the heart of gender inequality in the workplace is the unequal division of unpaid work between men and women. What is called 'time use data' from the ONS (the wonderful Office for National Statistics) points to little shift in the gender disparity, with women still doing 60% more unpaid caring work than men.[16]

According to a commission report on achieving a gender-equal economy by the Women's Budget Group, women aged 26 to 35 undertake the most unpaid work (34.6 hours on average per week compared with 17.4 hours for men in the same age group), suggesting that inequalities in unpaid work open up around the birth of the first child. By the age of 50, the report suggests that the gender disparity for care is most marked, with the responsibility of caring for ageing parents falling primarily on women.[17]

Unpaid work is of course vital to the functioning of society and the economy, and feminist economists (why just 'feminist' economists you might ask?) have long argued for it to be recognized on a par with paid work in systems of national accounting. Partly as a result of such campaigns, the ONS now publishes 'satellite household accounts' that value, in monetary terms, unpaid work. The most recent estimate put the total value of unpaid work at £1.24 trillion, larger in size than the UK's non-financial corporation sector, or the equivalent to 63% of GDP.[18] Over £1 trillion?!

I'm not suggesting that expectations of care and gendered role sharing, including the effect on retention and promotion, are ignored, as many organizations are making huge strides to adjust their maternity/paternity policies to reflect the need for equality. The fact that paternity leave is not taken up, with men returning to work facing the same issues as women have done for decades, is the subject of another book! What I am suggesting is that there is no recognition of the effect of care needs on the midlife female population. I asked every woman I interviewed for their organization's policy on care, and specifically caring for parents, or caring challenges faced by older workers. Not a single interviewee could give me a policy – moreover I was faced with blank stares, 'I don't know', 'I doubt that exists', 'let me think about that one', or 'that's a good idea'. This is a crazy omission given the prominence of caring at this life stage, and the influence on the otherwise upwards trajectory for the midlife woman's professional career.

Why women still can't have it all

Anne-Marie Slaughter, previously the first female director of policy planning for the US State Department, serving under Hillary Clinton, revived a national debate in 2012 with her article in *The Atlantic*, 'Why women still can't have it all'.[19] She proposed that, for women to be mothers and top professionals required either superhuman powers, being wealthy (to employ staff), or self-employed. Or having no children. She stepped back from her top position and received reactions ranging from disappointed, to condescending. She describes the penny dropping about the issues of 'having it all':

> *All my life, I'd been on the other side of this exchange. I'd been the woman smiling the faintly superior smile while another woman told me she had decided to take some time out or pursue a less competitive career track so that she could spend more time with her family. I'd been the woman congratulating herself on her unswerving commitment to the feminist cause, chatting smugly with her dwindling number of college or law-school friends who had reached and maintained their place on the highest rungs of their profession. I'd been the one telling young women at my lectures that you can have it all and do it all, regardless of what field you are in. Which means I'd been part, albeit unwittingly, of making millions of women feel that they are to blame if they cannot manage to rise up the ladder as fast as men and also have a family and an active home life (and be thin and beautiful to boot).*

I would love to disagree. I would like to shout from the top of a building, 'of course we can have it all! Look, the world's changed in the last decade!', but my learning shows this is still hard work for women, and particularly so for women at midlife when you add the multiplicity of care into the mix. Raya, a senior social worker, who at 55 was headhunted for two senior academic roles in the social work arena, describes this much better than I can:

> *This presented a dilemma for me, as at that time I was up to my eyes in caring issues for my father and sister. My sister has always had mental health problems, followed by brain damage from a coma, but she also had breast cancer, a double mastectomy and was very, very ill. So that was going on, and my father was diagnosed with Parkinson's and slowly but surely went downhill, until he was ultimately bedridden. At the same time my husband was ill. He had three major surgeries in three years. So at a time when I might have put my head up career-wise, I had to keep my head down. But then the stress of coping with my dad, sister, husband and keep my existing job meant that I was getting ill. So I took a three-month break to recharge and get everything in order. I ran one last workshop in London, then collapsed. I've had ME (myoencephalitis) for two years now.*

And what does your future career look like for you Raya?

> *When you are caring for others, and working full-time, you keep doing it because you sort of have to, and you keep digging in and you dig deeper and deeper and deeper and then one day you put your hand in the bucket and there isn't anything left. It just precipitated a physiological breakdown. And if I think it was about five plus years in the building up to, maybe it is going to take me five plus years to get to the other side of it. Then I'll think about my future career again.*

Burden or blessing?

I want to end this chapter with a rejoinder to the word 'burdensome' that's consistently used whenever the care of our children, parents, or family comes up. Particularly so with elderly parents, as adults traverse the country answering their urgent calls. In all of my discussions over the last five years with midlife women, one of the biggest reasons that women leave their roles is because they *want* to care for their parents. Yes, it's difficult, yes, it's emotional, yes, there is commonly a temporary trade-off with your career, but there is an acknowledgement that this is the only time left with them, and you're going to grab it, and enjoy it. I have so many sentences in my notebooks along the lines of 'I wouldn't change it for the world', 'I chose to do this', 'this was the only time I had left with her'.

I'll leave the last word to Samira, 55, who worked in public service as a senior manager, and gave up work to look after her mum who was diagnosed with rapid ovarian cancer.

> *Initially they were quite supportive, but in the end they decided they couldn't support me any further and withdrew my work contract. My mum took four months to die. My dad unfortunately took a turn for the worse just after mum died and died seven weeks later. Yes, at 55, I'm struggling to find a new job, this is not an easy age, but I don't regret it at all, I'd do it all over again to have that time with my mum and dad. It was a blessing. It was magical.*

CHAPTER 7

FACING MORTALITY

Death anxiety underlies much executive behavior and action.

(Manfred Kets de Vries, Professor of Leadership Development and Organizational Change, INSEAD)[1]

There was something unusually glib in Kristin's answer to my question as to why she walked away from her organization: 'Quite frankly, I was bored.'

Kristin had recently made the decision to leave her role as HR director of a media organization in order to complete her master's degree and start a PhD. This was a substantial career change, given that she had recently been appointed to the board. On the face of it, tedium was offered as the reason for the change in career, but as the interview progressed, the act of turning 50, and 'turning towards death', was uppermost in her mind:

Life is finite, which I know sounds ridiculous because the only thing we all share is the fact that death is inevitable. But I think it's that sense of when you're younger time just stretches out before you, and you know it's infinite, and I think when I hit 50 it was very much about 'actually at some point I'm going to get old and I'm not ready for that'.

She describes her shift out of her corporate role as 'self-indulgent' yet 'better than the alternative'. What does this mean? What's the alternative? Kristin revealed that the death of her mother at 54 underpinned her decision making (Kristin is 53), as 'she didn't get to enjoy this part of life':

> *In the next 20 years I shall be 70 and that feels old and I'm not quite ready. I've got lots more to do yet. I'm not ready to start the slow road to decline, I've got energy and I want an adventure and the adventure takes different shapes and forms. My PhD is an adventure.*

Kristin was one of my earliest interviews and I remember being surprised in listening back to our conversation by how significant the concept of mortality was to her decision making. Her notion of the 'slow road to decline' suggests she has been offered a direct reminder of the inevitability of death, which she is rejecting. Min, whom we'll meet later, viscerally describes: 'Oh my god! I'm only 20 years away from being in the same state as my parents.' Both of Min's parents have dementia.

The stealth motivator

This conversation about facing mortality at midlife – and the impact on career decisions – is a critical one. In my research, it was another one of the facets of life that contributed to women leaving their organizations. Not always the sole reason, but when combined with menopause, parental care, children's mental health or their own health issues, it became significant. It's the conversation that I'm sure any reader around the age of 50 will recognize having in private with friends. But it's not a conversation that is had in any business I know of. When someone is asked in an exit interview why they are leaving, they are likely to cite one the three most offered reasons: my manager (is a pain in the a***); my salary (isn't good enough); or new opportunities (someone else wants me). It's unlikely to be, 'oh, you know, I'm staring death in the face and I'm terrified'.

You'd think that organizational psychologists would be all over this subject, with hundreds of interested papers, debates, and reports on this, but you'd be wrong. As employee motivation has always been one of the key themes in management and leadership textbooks, you'd expect death anxiety to be included. Surprisingly, it's not. I can find fewer than ten papers, which you can guess by now are written by men, for men, using mainly male case studies! They are none the less important, and organizational psychologist Manfred Kets de Vries leads the field. Over a period of 40 years, he has urged the business world to take midlife, midlife reckoning and the fear of death seriously.[2] In his earliest paper, in 1978, 'The midcareer conundrum', his writing feels surprisingly contemporary:[3]

When people reach the midpoint of their lives a number of changes occur. Although the environment still seems full of opportunities, the preoccupation with inner life becomes more important. There is a greater sense of introspection, self-evaluation, and reflection. We notice an existential questioning of self, values, and life. There is a sudden awareness that we are growing older, that more than half our lives has already been lived. For some this leads to a sense of depression, for others it will heighten the commitment to make life more meaningful.

Humans are said to be unique in that we adapt and run our lives in the full knowledge not only of beginnings, but also of endings. But our anxiety about death causes a great degree of (conscious or unconscious) discomfort that manifests itself in a variety of emotional, cognitive, and direct actions. By 2014, Kets de Vries was writing about the 'stealth motivator', one of those phrases that pleasingly encapsulates a profound issue with two words.[4]

Death anxiety is a primary motivational force that drives much of our behavior. It puts our defenses on high alert, and we make strenuous efforts to repress or deny the unwelcome truth of our inevitable end. The way each of us denies death not only affects life in its broadest sense but also influences the way we behave in organizations. However, traditional motivational theories do not acknowledge the influence of death anxiety – The Stealth Motivator – on our behavior. Although they attempt to help us better understand employee motivation, they are not sufficiently inclusive.

Fundamentally, Kets de Vries is bringing the American cultural anthropologist Ernest Becker's seminal 1973 work on 'The denial of death' into the organizational world.[5] Winner of the Pulitzer Prize in 1974, Becker states: 'the fear of death is indeed a universal in the human condition... it makes wonderfully clear and intelligible, human actions that we have buried under mountains of fact and obscured with endless arguments about "true" human motives'.

Whilst Kets de Vries does not demarcate the experience of middle-aged men from that of women, he suggests this motivation is particularly important in the debate surrounding the career decisions of executives at midlife, who are more likely to experience loss, including the death of a parent or a friend, the departure of children from the parental home, traumatic life events (such as the pandemic), experiencing a 'big' birthday, or the influence of 'body mortality' – that is, the heightened awareness of the ageing body. He suggests that, when combined with menopause, death anxiety can affect midlife women more than men. This would make sense particularly in the last few years, with middle-aged women picking up the care of the extended family during and after the coronavirus pandemic, and facing death on a regular basis, whether seeing it on TV or, unfortunately, within their family or friendship circle.

And certainly these potential gender differences are echoed in my study, with middle-aged women intimately connected with the care of their parents, feeling the loss of their 'empty nest', recognizing the end of their fertility, and noticing (or being reminded of) the effects of time and age on their mortal bodies. The so-called 'stealth motivator', or our ability to look ahead, is the steep price we pay for our development as a species. As Kets de Vries describes,

> burdened with the cognitive/emotive capacity of knowing about our own inevitable demise makes us fearful of what lies ahead. Among the uncertainties of what's coming in the future is one dread certainty, and this puts our armoury of defences on high alert.[6]

Avoiding the 'nasties'

This sense of threat is evident in Nora's description of her current career state. Having recently left her role as CEO of an entertainment complex, Nora, 60, has already embarked on setting up three further companies, one with a previous colleague, one with her son and another as an angel investor. She is close to her mother whom she describes as a 'ball of energy', which is a great description of Nora herself, who, far from slowing down, feels like she is speeding up:

> I do slightly wrack myself as to whether actually I'm making myself busier. The idea was that I would ease back a little bit, but the trouble is everything is so interesting, so lots of entrepreneurial things that keep happening and I keep being offered things and I think 'ohhh, that'll be fun'.

Nora identifies strongly with her mother and it is this act of identification, and of watching her mother care for her stepfather, that appears to be driving a capacity for work; her desire for change and her need to 'make the most' of this time of life. She uses the word 'dread' and potential 'nasties' throughout the interview:

> *I'm more like my mother really. So, I'm watching my mother and how hard she's finding it with my 87-year-old stepfather, he's nearly blind now and he's very doddery, and that's stopped them being able to go abroad and on holidays. They're trapped in their house quite a lot, and all those sort of things, and I think 'oh God, what if I'm going to be like that as well? That's a definite dread.'*

Furthermore, Nora translates this fear to her own life:

> *I have an unspoken dread here. That is, that I'm going to end up looking after my partner. I'm coming up 60 he's 64. When you see people who are tied into having to look after their spouse and it's part of the promise, and I have an absolute dread of that.*

What is particularly pertinent about this exchange is how Nora, by facing into the threshold of mortality, extrapolates her mother's current experience into her own potential experience, and uses this understanding to make future decisions:

> *I need to grab my time and I need to organize my work around the possibility that this will start happening, which makes you think one should simplify one's life sooner rather than later so that not too much falls over. Because nasty bits of news do happen to us now in our late 50s and early 60s. Lots of my friends and peers are having those sorts of hospital visits, and there's the nasties coming on and one starts to attend more funerals.*

The ticking clock

As Nora suggests, it is apparent that the losses, fears, and changes surrounding the threshold of the middle years act as a spur for future change and growth – what she describes as the 'ticking clock'. The notion of time has become a visceral concept, giving the perception of urgency and necessity that might fuel a future direction. James Hollis, a psychodynamic therapist and author of the startling book, *The Middle Passage*, talks about time.[7] He reminds his readers that the 'middle passage' is less a chronological event than a psychological experience, using the two Greek words for 'time', *chronos* and *kairos*, to observe this distinction. *Chronos* is sequential, linear time. It's quantifiable and many of us spend our lives worrying about whether we have enough of it, whether we're losing it, running out of it, or being consumed by it. *Chronos* time, it seems, will eat us alive if we don't constantly keep track of it and try to control it, by every digital or paper means possible! In contrast, *kairos* is the qualitative time of life. The Greeks considered it the most appropriate dimension for something new. To grasp *kairos* time we have to release some of our anxiety around *chronos* time, for example, trusting that such a simple act of self-care is anything but a waste of time. For Hollis, our middle passage occurs when a person is obliged to view their life as something more than a linear succession of years. As he suggests:

> *The longer one remains unconscious, which is quite easy to do in our culture, the more likely one is to see life only as a succession of moments leading toward some vague end, the purpose of which will become clear in due time. When one is stunned into consciousness, one's life span is rendered in a depth perspective: who am I, then, and whither bound?*

Time as a theme echoes across the interviews. Often this concept is described wistfully, in the past tense, in that it has 'flown by' (Kristin). But more commonly it is described urgently, as a future need that one must grab hold of, for, as Chris somewhat wistfully notes, 'we haven't got many summers left'. Or, as Min states,

The recognition you have of mortality, and that suddenly you're like, 'oh, jeez, I'm more than halfway through my life'. That suddenly hits you, and it's bizarre. Your life seems to suddenly hit you.

For other respondents, this 'ticking clock' is a looming presence, signifying potential danger. For example, Ines describes the anxiety she and her siblings are experiencing watching their parents deteriorate health-wise: 'It's like watching a timer, but you just don't know if a potential health crisis will be in a year's time, five years' time or ten years' time.' More commonly, in an uncannily similar way to the so-called biological clock that ticks away for many women, the threshold of midlife is a phase that signals the need for change, as Chris poignantly states:

I'm running out of time, running out of earning potential, running out of who wants you.

Mirror, mirror on the wall

Manfred Kets de Vries states that 'body mortality' is a major signifier of the 'stealth motivator', and throughout the interviews, women offered visceral examples of 'staring death in the face' through facing their own, and others' ageing bodies.

Ana looks at the 'frumpy' photos of her mother at 50 and rejects this image for herself, ensuring she follows strict disciplines for her own body, weight, hair, clothes, and exercise regime. Frances describes 'pounding' her body at the gym, to avoid her mum's experience:

My mum was crippled with arthritis at a very young age, so when I was in university she was in a wheelchair, but her immunity was never checked, but that's why I'm so adamant that I'm going to keep fit.

Both Min's parents have dementia, driving a need to stay fit: 'I've got to look after myself cos I don't want vascular dementia and so I get to the gym'. And if not parents, midlife is the age when the possibility exists for 'stuff starting to go wrong' for one's peer group, as Eve suggests:

> *I feel really fit, really healthy and pretty robust actually and am amazingly grateful for that. I have been very free from illness, scares, but a lot of my colleagues, friends, are starting to have cancer. I kind of let this in a bit, and then I go and do a boot camp and maybe drink a bit less wine and think 'thank god it's not me'.*

Of course, not everyone described their ageing bodies in positive terms or intended to discipline their bodies into a fitter form. For a small number of respondents, they openly described their ageing body as a site of disgust ('hideous... horrible body'), at one extreme, or treated it with humorous ambivalence at the other. In Evans' 2017 book, *The Persistence of Gender Inequality*, she describes 21st-century woman gazing despondently into the mirror, suggesting the world in which this woman lives is one of ruthless self-examination and social expectations.[8] There is an urgency to Meg's comment:

> *I want to look in the mirror and not shrink in horror and that requires me to maintain a certain weight. That's my goal. To maintain a certain weight and I know I can do that. I know I can do that and I will.*

Or as Marie, 51, says: 'I still feel young until I look in the mirror'. Or Chris adds: 'I notice my age because I catch myself in that lift in the mirror... Bags under my eyes, lines on my face, I don't like it, so I don't look.' Min describes the toilet scene at work: 'It's funny, you go to the loos here and women of a certain age are doing that (pulling skin from face back) we're all doing that, pulling the skin back slightly.'

Bel's experience is more intimate. At 50, rising through the ranks of property management, she describes herself as being 'braver personally, professionally, physically than I've ever been despite my ME', recently taking on a personal trainer, which she describes as 'life changing'. I was curious as to the timing of this:

> *Why now? This will sound a bit weird I think, but because I'm not dead. There was a real possibility of this. I mean I was really ill at one point and fainting like ten times a day. I was trying to work and it was horrendous, but I was determined and I didn't used to get much warning because I was learning, so I'd be flailing about and knocking things over and crashing into things, but I kept working in the main. It was scary.*

You kept working full-time through this period of illness, Bel?

> *Of course. My dad had died when he was my age, and I've lost a lot of people young and I think it's that.*

And like a shot, we're back to the 'stealth motivator', the death anxiety causing an impact on midlife women's career decisions. Or, put another way, one of the prevailing collisions that can occur in midlife and colour the choices we make. It's worth noting that this realization of facing mortality is not inevitably negative. It can be fascinating and thought-provoking. It can be tender, poignant and a moment for reflection. Perhaps, the tipping point for change. Or the start of the revolution! Read on, as there is much hope to be realized in the next section!

PART 3

REVOLUTION

For I conclude that the enemy is not lipstick, but guilt itself; we deserve lipstick, if we want it, AND free speech; we deserve to be sexual AND serious – or whatever we please. We are entitled to wear cowboy boots to our own revolution.

(Naomi Wolf, *The Beauty Myth*, 1991)

CHAPTER 8

MOTIVATION AND MIDLIFE

Probably the happiest period in life most frequently is in middle age, when the eager passions of youth have cooled, and the infirmities of age not yet begun; as we see that the shadows, which are at morning and evening so large, almost entirely disappear at midday.

(Eleanor Roosevelt)

It's very easy to research the difficulties faced by professional middle-aged women and get stuck in the midst of problematic data of power imbalance, caring challenges, and midlife collisions. I'm reminded of the moment in my PhD exam, when my examiner, the gifted Professor Susan Vinnicombe, said, 'Thank goodness for your section on Revolt, Lucy. I was beginning to worry your PhD was just going to be about the problems midlife women face. You've given me hope'! This is the woman who has championed gender equality for a decade at Cranfield University, rigorously holding organizations to account for their progress – or lack of progress – through her annual Female FTSE Reports, and she was right.

Because there is a different conversation to be had here too in this book. A hopeful and celebratory conversation, led by stories of self-determined growth, resilience, and ambition, of female 'revolt', and how women at midlife can accept their vulnerability and embrace a turning point in their lives. I'd go further and suggest that it's *because* so many midlife women face challenge and loss in their professional and personal lives, they are able to articulate and recognize what they do not wish to be, that is, 'not me', and embark on the next chapter of their lives with vigour. These are women who possess energy, creativity, and exceptional resilience. Qualities any organization should be queuing up for!

To stop, to pause, to change

After the breathlessness of midlife events, for many midlife women there is an experience of a turning point, a moment in time where the need is, as Lori says, 'to stop, to pause, to change'. There is something particularly potent and poignant about the questions posed by so many of my interviewees that chime with earlier themes, that is: facing into mortality; the notion of time being 'squeezed'; and the parallel shifting of priorities. Women reflect on meaning, belonging and the sense-making of midlife. Kristin poses herself multiple questions about meaning:

> *If I only have four years left, like my mum did unbe-knownst to her, what would I want to do? What does it mean to be 50? In the next 20 years, you're going to be 70, so what does that mean and what will your health be like?… Will you be mobile and will [her husband] still be alive?… What do I want to be known for, what do I want to stand for?*

Nora, recently divorced, is wistful about belonging:

> *And then my immediate family were very angry when we got divorced. My eldest son said, 'you know that we're a small family and what have you done?' So, the other thing about being this age, this is a key one actually, is 'who do I belong to?'*

The challenge that could be levelled at midlife women goes, 'Well, if you're so ambitious, why did you walk away from your organization?' The most obvious answer is that, faced with impossible work/life collisions, there was no choice. But what isn't discussed, or recognized by so many corporations, is the temporality of events women face at midlife. This is much more radical than it sounds. Because after the storm comes the calm. Or, put another way, for the middle-aged woman, after the storm comes the revolution! And I mean revolution in its broadest sense – a turnaround, a change, a revival, a rethink, a freshness. And not only this, but a motivation to live with energy, meaning, and purpose.

The three phases of midlife

It occurs to me there are three phases at midlife for many women:

Phase 1: To stop. The time of crisis, when all the pressures come together.

Phase 2: To pause. To press pause on the career, to care, to cope, to look 'inwards'.

Phase 3: To change. To rethink, to look 'outwards', to wonder 'what next' and embrace newness.

You might remember Nina in Chapter 6, who found herself at midlife with two teenage children still at home, a difficult menopausal experience, a full-time job, whilst also caring for her mother, aunt, and mother-in-law. This is a time in her life she described as 'just unbelievable, full on, disturbing and very, very hard'. At this stage Nina was in Phase 1. A time of crisis. During Phase 2, Nina pressed pause on her career. She didn't step out of her company, but certainly didn't pursue the opportunity to step up in her career at this point in her life, stating 'I didn't feel it was an option… with all the responsibility'. By the time of our interview, Nina, 54, was in Phase 3 and actively pursuing her next career chapter: 'I'm Head of Learning and Development now, managing 24 centres across nine countries and I absolutely love it. I can now travel. I am not restrained now.' Her three older relatives have died, and her children, whilst still at home, are more independent. She describes her life:

> *They're all gone now. And obviously I miss them, but actually you go through that, and now I have time to enjoy a different kind of life. I think my life has been either working and studying, or working and children, or working and caring. And I think that really the last couple of years have just been about me, about us. Which has been really nice.*

The fact that 'time passes' might seem obvious, yet, when the workplace is taken into consideration, so many sudden career decisions are made in Phases 1 and 2 of a woman's midlife that have profound consequences on the future. How different it might be if reflection time was built into these phases to enable women to stay in, or return to, their jobs.

But reflection time – or even a moment to breathe and take stock of the next chapter – is not built into the make-up of the patriarchal organization, which demands of its leaders a full-time dedication and preoccupation, following a linear pathway with no uncertainty. Yet, contrary to much of the lifespan literature or organizational design, the need to reflect and consider one's life's journey does not necessarily correlate with the desire to step out or retire. Far from it, as critical to this book is how many of the respondents describe the desire for greater flexibility and work/life balance, *in order* to enable their ambition.

Julia Kristeva is a Bulgarian-French philosopher whose work inspired me for years and caused me to consider the nature of women's search for meaning and revolt against the status quo. She suggests that 'revolt has always meant a turning in time, space and kind, suggesting different forms of social political and ethical transformation',[1] and she has spent much of her life calling for a revolution in organizations and society, not so much a political one, as a cultural and psychological one. She appreciated writers and artists who dedicated their lives to thinking and uncovering meaning in their lives, defining revolt as the ability 'to call things into question'. As she states, 'To think is to revolt. Meaning is revolt.'[2] Nora articulates the need for space and time to reflect:

> *By the time you're a 50-year-old woman, it's all about time, it's all about wanting time, it's all about wanting time enough to pause, so that I'm ready to come back again. I think a lot of women in their 50s and 60s are feeling that, so if only organizations can give people time.*

Jude's story is interesting in that she is the only person I interviewed who had left a senior role within a blue-chip organization, taken a year out ('the best thing I ever did'), and returned to a different organization, stepping up to a board director role:

> *Yes, I previously had lots of responsibility, a big team, but after a venture capitalist takeover, an all-male new team, my face didn't fit. It was hard to leave, I'd been there 17 years and was all-encompassing, and I had no idea what to do next. So I took a break. I retrained as a coach, learned a lot about myself and what I could have done differently, or better in my previous role.*

Through her network, Jude at 48 was offered a substantial leadership role two years later (and after nursing her partner through cancer).

> *It's a big role, on the Board and probably double, treble the responsibility I had before. It's quite different starting again, with a brand-new executive team who are a new*

team themselves, with a new environment, different challenges.

She's quite clear that her ability to accept the challenge and make the step up is due to her time out from organizational life:

Funny, I don't feel fazed by it at all, and I think the break has taught me a lot, that I can do it. The opportunity with this role was to prove it really. Not to anybody else, just to myself.

The career clock

This desire for change, Phase 3, can differ substantially between men and women. It's worth repeating from the first chapter, that 70% of the women in my study were ready to step up in their careers, within or without their current organizations, offering proactive tales of energy and ambition – often thwarted by the organization and channelled into self-employment. We need to challenge the prevalent, 50-year-old, business motivation and lifespan assumptions, that dictate that 'life after midlife' is one of stagnation, retirement, golf courses, and general decline, or just one of vocation and giving back. Of course it might be all of this (or some of this for some women), but the basis of all of these midlife motivation theories stems from male scientists, basing their theories on the male foundation stones of a linear full-time career, ebbing away into decline after midlife.[3]

I've only found one theorist who comes close to describing the experience I heard from so many women: David Karp, who, after interviewing midlife professionals, wrote a paper noting a significant difference between the genders at approximately 50 years.[4] He suggested that men at this stage begin to develop an 'exiting consciousness', whilst women are still striving to make their mark. He stated, 'for the most part, the women interviewed are being "turned on" at the same age that their male counterparts are considering whether to "turn off"'.

I'm so intrigued by this notion and I call it the 'career clock', which I'm convinced ticks differently for men and women. What if achievement doesn't decline at middle age? What if it could be a peak period for competence, mastery, career satisfaction, and empowerment? What if women, having spent their lives in so-called 'squiggly' careers,[5] come into their own after midlife? What if men and women at midlife just have different career clocks – the male one shifting into a cosy 8pm late evening at midlife, the female one ticking into 3pm with so much to do by teatime! This is supported by research by Judith Gordon and Karen Whelan who differentiated the motivation between women and men at midlife, suggesting that the 'unrecognized differences between midlife women and midlife men have contributed to a lack of organizational and societal support for an effective midcareer for women'.[6] Albeit some 20 years old, this research remains resonant, highlighting important differences between the genders, with men confronting a personal psychological and life re-evaluation, whilst women are stepping into the notion of 'continued achievement, accomplishment and perceived value to the organization, relishing the challenge of work and needing the intellectual stimulation'.

Two American scientists, Connie Gersick and Kathy Kram, conducted research at the turn of the 21st century into high-achieving women at midlife.[7] This was such an unusual study at this time, it was labelled 'non-traditional research'! They found that midlife women experience a transition, a 'coming into one's own and gaining confidence in one's abilities, knowing what one wants and being able to go after it'. Additional research suggests that women gain in personal power, prestige, and influence as they grow older, and perceive themselves as intelligent, assertive, and determined, with the balance of interpersonal power in the latter half of women's lives increasing in favour of older women.[8] Midlife was deemed the age period during which (professional, middle-class) women were most empowered, having accomplished a great deal in their lives and with the education and knowledge to advocate successfully for themselves and others.

Skin in the game

So what arose in my study was a majority of women who want (or wanted) to stay within their profession or organization and move further up the career ladder – *despite* the considerable barriers of exclusion, caring responsibilities, and insistence on full-time work. Lori, whose story has been told in Chapter 4, describes herself as 'still very ambitious' and has every intention of returning to full-time work after the caring for her daughter and mother has stabilized. Gaynor is clear that, having fought to get where she has in the academic world, she is not stopping now:

> *I wouldn't actually want to give up my career. Why would I give it up now when I'm just probably through the glass ceiling? I've got there, I've got skin in the game, so I'm not going to give it up at the moment. I don't want to step back to being everybody's personal assistant (at home) which is what was expected of me before. Everything from people's care through to their dry cleaning, through to phone calls, through to anything was my job for the whole kit and caboodle. Now, people are starting to do things themselves and my partner's doing something. It's just great.*

And Frances, a corporate financier, confronts the gendered notion of retirement. At 55, she describes herself as having a 'zero tolerance to boredom' with no plans for retirement. Yet what she notices is how often people ask her when she intends to retire:

> *I think I've got to almost the offended stage, because when you reach a certain age, and you're a woman, people will say to you, 'oh when are you retiring?' And that conversation, that's come up more times recently than I think is comfortable. I don't believe the first thing people say to a man who is 55/56 is 'oh, so when are you retiring?'*

But so many of these vibrant women face the struggle to return to an organization, yet their desire to step up to full-time work remains undimmed. Niamh, 53, took an undesired break from her career in teaching, as she pursued an unfair dismissal case after being sacked (which she won). Despite a dent to her confidence during this period, she describes herself now as 'full of energy and life', with the legalities and her divorce behind her and wanting to step back up to a full-time career headship post. Gail, 61, previously held two UK-based full-time CEO roles. Unfortunately her mother became ill with 'locked-in syndrome' and the five years she spent caring for her prevented her from travelling. As a consequence, Gail moved into non-executive roles to manage the situation. After her mother died, she has been trying to return full-time to the workplace, describing herself as:

> *More energized and engaged about the exploration of this world than ever before. I think the future is open. There is a whole journey waiting for me. The future is definitely not 'not working'. I just want more of it really!*

One of the many assumptions about motivation at midlife is that the transition involves a shift towards giving back to others, towards meaning and to leaving a legacy for the next generation.[9] Whilst these are concepts mentioned by my respondents as important, I would (strongly!) suggest there is a gender bias in these assumptions. When women have spent their lives caring for others, it is perhaps a relief to take time for oneself. There are as many respondents who want to 'give back' and leave a legacy, as there are those who admit there is freedom in *not* caring and an enjoyment in looking out for yourself for once. As Min, a 53-year-old board director, says:

> *I'm used to fixing everything for everybody no matter who. Time to stop it now. We all need that little bit of confidence to say, 'actually, I need to look after myself now'. A lot of people have relied on me in the past and now needs to be an investment in me in the future.*

What shines out from the data is a desire from the respondents to offer alternative narratives to the culturally pervasive decline account. 'Progress narrative' is the term used by Margaret Gullette for 'stories in which the implicit meaning of aging runs from survival, resilience, recovery and development', insisting that people need to feel they can 'colonise the future with some degree of success'.[10] William Bridges' theory of transitions discusses renewal at any stage of life as the 'New Beginning',[11] and Julia Kristeva hails the ability of women 'to metamorphose, to reconstruct oneself, to be born again' as one of the factors of female 'genius'.[12] In the following two chapters, the nature (or sparkle!) of female midlife genius is explored, together with the ways in which women challenge prevailing myths and assumptions as they reflect, 'reconstruct' and reconfigure their lives at midlife, refusing to be defined by your, or anyone else's, narrow life trajectory.

CHAPTER 9

THE SPARKLE OF FEMALE GENIUS!

I always have a comfortable feeling that nothing is impossible if one applies a certain amount of energy in the right direction. When I want things done, which is always at the last moment, and I am met with such an answer: 'It's too late. I hardly think it can be done'; I simply say: 'Nonsense! If you want to do it, you can do it'.

(Nellie Bly, 1864–1922. In 1889, she set a world record for navigating the globe in 72 days, eight days less than Phileas Fogg)

In amidst Julia Kristeva's impenetrable philosophical papers, I remember reading this phrase, 'the sparkle of female genius', to describe the middle-aged woman, and thinking, yes! I can work with this. She describes women's

intoxication with life, their interest in the other. Contrary to what is often stated – they say women are narcissistic – I believe them to be less narcissistic than men, and they have a far stronger relationship to things outside of themselves, be it children, love relations, or social life.[1]

I wrote the phrase on a sticky note to remind myself when studying of my passion for this theme, and what I hoped other people would positively embrace about the subject – but more importantly, the subjects! What is the 'sparkle of female genius'? To me and to so many other middle-aged women, it's the female mindset that propels older women onwards and upwards; it's the difference that enables them to embrace both an achievement and a growth motivation; it's the difference that shines through as they hold all areas of their lives together – sometimes by a thread, but still hanging on. For an organization, the question is different. What is it that we, as an organization, want to do? And I hope the answer is to retain our midlife female talent because of that resilient sparkle!

'Not me' and midlife revolt

The so-called sparkle started with outright challenge. Almost every woman I interviewed resisted the terms I was using to describe my data set. Midlife, middle-aged, older women. No, no, no! 'You can interview me as long as you don't describe me as middle-aged', 'Older woman? Quite frankly, it's rude!' Ha! Why the challenge? Kristin says it well. She describes one of her many midlife motivations as 'bucking the trend', and her palpable frustration at the supposed myths surrounding women at midlife is shared by many women at this stage of life. They offer an astute awareness of the damage this language can cause not only to the individual, but also to the broader societal and cultural perception of, and action towards, older professional women. Claire is clear in her belief that the decline storyline can imbue women at midlife with a limited mindset, 'I think there is a lot of challenging to be done which is actually you don't have to do that, you don't have to be like that, you have choices'.

And Sandra is clear that the assumptions applied to older people simply standardize the ageing process:

> You can't assume the idea that just because you're older you stop wanting to change and challenge yourself. I know some people are like that, but I know people who are

20 years old who are like that. You just have to judge it by
the person.

Sandra, Claire, and Kristin are not alone in their frustration, with respondents in turn describing the lack of profession- al older women in business as an 'untapped resource', 'a waste of good talent' and 'a tragedy'. Min summarizes this frustration:

I think we have a way to go before we overturn the
society image about valuing the skills that women have
in middle age. We have so many skills and life skills and
professional expertise. We have learning knowledge that
we've collected like a bird's nest, and not to use that feels
like a waste.

This is not to say that the women I interviewed did not feel fear, worry, loss, or exclusion as part of their future story, but that the findings offered as much of a sense of joy, lib- eration and wonder in their experience of midlife. These respondents are women who describe midlife as a 'good age' and a 'lucky age', energized by 'exciting plans'. They appear ready to take on challenges, often seeming burst- ing with urgency and a vibrancy. And, as the respondents describe the benefits of middle age, the same positive, pro- active language is repeated by the majority: 'confidence... maturity... wisdom... experience... assertion... care less... speaking up... calmer... rational'.

Revelling in post-menopausal zest!

This sense of liberation, motivation, and confidence appears to go hand in hand with a turning point away from the chaos of midlife collision. Or as Margaret Mead famously stated in *Life* magazine in 1959, 'there is no greater power or creative force in the world than the zest of a postmenopausal woman'.[2] She defined post-menopausal zest as a 'physical and psychological surge of energy'. Margaret Mead was a renowned American anthropologist, and for all the innumerable ways that this intriguing woman pioneered modern thought on sex and gender theory, this statement was particularly radical. Particularly as 70 years later, it's still headline news when a woman heads up a business or seizes a cultural moment after the age of 50. On a David Frost show in the 1970s, Mead again publicly attributed her energy to her post-menopausal zest, a sensation that, some 50 years later, still has limited acknowledgement in research. This recognition of post-menopausal zest offers another factor in the rise of the 'achievement' motivation in later life for professional midlife women. In my study, the majority of respondents recognized the difficulties they experienced during peri-menopause and menopause as temporary, as Meg's comment suggests as she reflects on this period of her life: 'But it passes [the difficult symptoms of the menopause]. Those moments are just moments. They don't define you and they are not forever.' Sandra, 64, is positively buoyant about her post-menopausal self:

> *That's something else I think people don't recognize about this age is that your children leave home, you overcome the worse effects of the menopause and you feel absolutely fantastic. So, I'm relieved of lots of the issues and I actually think people in my age feel very good.*

And many women on the other side of menopause will be the first to advocate for a shift in societal mindset. For all the upheaval of peri-menopause and the weight the hormonal changes can carry, there are studies that agree with my findings and suggest that after menopause, our emotional state isn't just unscathed – it thrives. As of today, I can find only four studies that explore the rise and fall of optimism through adulthood, and they're consistent in their conclusions:[3] essentially, optimism follows a U-shape trajectory, climbing steadily from 51 to 70 years, and only then stabilizing. Even more fascinating is that this upwards curve is obviously enhanced by positive life events, but not derailed by negative life events.

This is not to say that a natural post-menopausal 'upsurge' is every woman's experience. Many of the women I interviewed were aware of the need to consciously, and positively, shift their mindset to the next phase of their life. Jude, for instance, whose difficult peri-menopausal experience was highlighted in Chapter 5, is beset by familial and medical advice: 'Everybody keeps saying you are only at the start of your menopause, and then I go, "oh my god if I'm only at the start, bloody hell, God help me"…' But she is clear as to her choices for her post-menopausal life:

> My mother-in-law said she felt really old (after the menopause) and that was it, that was the end of her use. I don't feel like that at all. I feel the absolute opposite of that. However difficult now, I think it is the next stage of my life and that'll be really good. You have got to see it as a positive. I want to work my way through it and be proud to be through it.

The prevalent negative menopause media publicity of depression, brain fog, and general incapacity was discussed by a number of respondents, who reflected on their choice to either 'conform' or break stereotype. Having ME (myalgic encephalomyelitis) and holding down a senior manager role, Bel is used to being pathologized in the workplace and throughout her interview discussed her motivation to challenge assumptions of her capability. This is useful learning for her as she faces her post-menopausal self:

I am worried about what the media says about (menopausal) women – they aren't able to perform, and their brain doesn't work as well. That panics me a bit but then I thought, well okay but people have said different things over the years, people wrote me off with ME, 'you're not going to be able to do a job like that with ME' and I have. So, stereotypes are there to be broken not conformed to.

Given what Min describes as 'the syntax that suggests you should just give up', it is unsurprising how keen respondents were to stress that their minds were as sharp (or sharper) than in their younger years. This is really important as there is so much emphasis on the menopausal woman being mentally weaker than her younger peers – or the men.

Every time I read reports about the brain-fogged middle-aged woman, I want the authors to read my interviews! As Kristin studies for her PhD, and Cyn for her master's, Gaynor describes herself as still having the 'intellectual edge'. Sandra is 'fizzing with lots of ideas'; Niamh is 'more mentally alert' and Gail believes the menopause has given her a 'mental sharpness that I didn't have before'. The conversations women were having with me were in direct contrast to what you might think. Everyone was keen to talk about pushing physical and mental boundaries, about staying alert and sharp, and approaching life with vim and vigour. There is a liberation in their talk, not just an emancipation from their reproductive body but also from spending a lifetime caring what others think of their minds, of their bodies, of their motivation. 'Shackles off', says Kathy! There is a self-deprecating humour in most middle-aged women, who are so used to being looked at, examined, and judged at work. I laugh every time I read Min's comment, 'I can go to the gym and literally I could run around naked and nobody would bat an eyelid. Invisible, but liberated in my invisibility!'

From 'erotic capital' to 'grey capital'

Psychologists and social scientists are pretty obsessed with the different forms of 'capital' held by groups and individuals. For example, many schoolboys leave their famous public schools with a built-in 'social capital' – a network that provides relational ties they can leverage for life. 'Human capital' refers to the skills and abilities a company's employees bring to the operation, and 'psychological capital' is the ability to strengthen our personal resources of hope and optimism. And then there is 'erotic capital' (we looked at this concept in Chapter 2), a phrase coined by academic Catherine Hakim, which supposedly endows a beautiful, sexually attractive, and vivacious young woman with power and influence.[4]

I am either being naïve or revolutionary here (I'll take the latter!) to propose the concept of 'grey capital' for women. It's not a term that exists, although it's certainly prevalent for the grey-haired man. Just think of the influential silver foxes that are George Clooney, Idris Elba, Barack Obama, Mark Ruffalo – you get my drift. Yes, stunning women like Helen Mirren, Jamie Lee Curtis, and Andie MacDowell are making headlines with their grey hair, but the emphasis is always on their hair, not their power and influence. In the business literature, the colour grey remains associated with problems (discussed in Chapter 2), think the 'grey tsunami' of the ageing population.

So grey hair might not (yet!) be associated with erotic power, but this very release of potential eroticism of the younger body liberates many older women. Far from regretting their (perceived) loss of looks or midlife invisibility, many women gain a freedom in midlife from the gendered and sexual selves they have spent much of their lives constructing, and a liberty in shedding the constant 'body work' of their younger selves. Or indeed, a freedom from the patriarchal workplace, where the ageing woman invests considerable time and energy to consistently prove her youthfulness.

Ulpukka Isopahkala-Bouret is a Professor in the Centre for Research on Lifelong Learning and Education at the University of Helsinki. Her research on middle-aged female executives reported that the increase in noticeable signs of ageing, coupled with the decrease in perceived sexuality, enabled the qualifications and competence of the older woman to be more visible.[5] That is, she concludes, professional authority and credibility can increase as a result of looking older. Wowzer, grey capital!

In discussing her decision to go grey, Eve describes this as a 'significant marker in her professional career'. As she became sidelined in her leadership role within the NHS, due in part she believes to the perception of her as an 'older aunt', she became, 'in spectacular contrast', of huge value in her private counselling practice.

> *My age, my looks, offers a sense of wisdom and being unshockable. They can open up, it's not a problem. In the safety of the consulting room, age is absolutely on my side and, what is wonderful, is I feel that this will only increase.*

'Braver, stronger, fitter': loss and gain

As I sit back and re-read my interviews, it is perhaps unsurprising the words 'resilience' and 'growth' were repeated so often. As discussed in Part 2, 'Collision', every woman I interviewed had faced varying degrees of loss and adversity, and significant change, by this stage of their lives. At the same time, their lives were also shored up by experience and learning, a sense of control, perceived social support, and some balance and perspective – all protective factors that enable resilience, particularly in high achievers.[6]

Robin, whose husband has been ill for some 20 years, uses similar words:

Some days I think I've got such a wealth of experience, and it helps me to deal with life and what's thrown at me. I think, 'wow, if I were a lot younger I don't think I'd have the resilience or the flexibility to be able to just shut things off' which is what I tend to do. So, I keep things in boxes. If I were a lot younger I wouldn't have the mindset or the understanding that that is the way to cope with it, for sure.

And Robin is not an isolated example. Niamh, for example, who has recently won a lawsuit for unfair dismissal and is coping with her divorce, discusses 'bouncing back' from adversity:

Obviously the stuff around the job and marriage break up was stressful but actually you push through it. People say, 'oh you coped really well' and I think, well at least I've got my parents, and my children are settled, at least I'm working, so there was always the kind of the upside to things. I don't dwell. I mean there are times when I think this is really shitty, but I always think, 'I've got this', and 'I can always do this'.

But the nature of resilience is so much more than just the ability to develop psychological and behavioural capabilities that enable survival through crises, or put another way, to function almost normally despite the crisis or change. It is also about growth through, and beyond, loss and adversity. That is, resilience allows a person to rebound from adversity as a strengthened and more resourceful person. This is a new strand of research that runs parallel to that of post-traumatic stress, and the phenomenon is labelled 'post-traumatic growth'.[7] Over the last 20 years (with a resurgence of research post-pandemic), scientists have learned that negative events – such as the collision that midlife women often experience – can spur positive change. This includes a recognition of personal strength, the exploration of new possibilities, improved relationships, a greater appreciation for life and spiritual growth. Bel describes herself as 'braver, stronger, fitter' as she comes to terms with her ME:

> *I'm braver personally, professionally, and physically than I've ever been. I got so frustrated as my ME wrecks my balance, and I'd be falling over at work, sometimes ten times a day and trying to work full-time was horrendous. I'd be flailing around and knocking things over and crashing into people. I felt desperate and embarrassed. I'm so much more confident now. I'm determined and I don't want to be written off in any part of my life or not fulfil my potential. I now know that bad things happen to good people, regardless of planning and thinking you can protect yourself. I've got a personal trainer now and she's been absolutely life changing. Yes, there's days when I still tip over, but I don't beat myself up now. I just get back on the horse.*

And Lori, who is caring for her daughter and mother, suggests:

> *Yes, definitely, from all these challenges, and from a life point of view, I definitely feel wiser than I've ever felt before. I feel things have come far more intuitively just because I've done things before and I've got more experience under my belt. I feel, as you know, as big and powerful as I have ever felt at any other point in my career and life.*

I love the underbelly of fire in these women's responses, a sense of 'taking on the world', staring the myths in the face and proving them wrong. I'm struck by the language of challenge and fight; of pushing and passion – of which Frances is a good example:

All the time in my career when I've been undermined, belittled, taken for granted, I will use it to my advantage. I've always been very positive about what I want and if people underestimate me, that's their problem not mine. Those people that know me certainly don't ever pat me on the head unless they want it bitten off! If it looks as if I'm comfortable in my slippers, that's not the case, because everything I do is a challenge. Nobody drives me, nobody's got a whip out there saying 'Frances, find the next deal'. I do this to myself because I'm self-driven and still excited.

What we are looking at here is data that supports evidence of an *increase* of motivation for many professional women at midlife, fuelled by the abating of difficult physical, emotional, and familial circumstances that, in turn, drives a resilience and desire for growth. The significant study by Noon into the lives of women aged 45–60 (highlighted in Chapter 4), that found 50% of the 2,000 respondents experiencing five or more traumatic life events by midlife, is important here. Because the study is keen to stress that it is the women who have been through the fire, or 'forged by fire', who are now confident, happy, and solid in their lives.[8]

Many women acknowledge the decline narrative, whilst rejecting it ('not me') in favour of a 'progress' narrative that offers a more positive and energizing story, with space for an ambitious future. Yet at the same time, respondents are challenging the meaning of achievement and ambition in today's workplace, desiring, in the main, a flexibility that appears limited for professional female executives. So, there is a call for a reconfiguration – in language and practice – of how achievement is recognized and enabled in the workplace, examined further in the next chapter.

CHAPTER 10

REWRITING THE RULES OF CAREER SUCCESS

You have to make more noise than anybody else, you have to make yourself more obtrusive than anybody else, you have to fill all the papers more than anybody else, in fact you have to be there all the time and see that they do not snow you under, if you are really going to get your reform realised.

(Emmeline Pankhurst, 1858–1928)

What is common across my data of midlife women and their career ambitions is three factors:

1. Their enjoyment and innate interest in work.
2. Their desire for flexibility from an organization to give them space to 'feed all areas of their lives', thus achieving a sustainable work/life balance.
3. Their ability to grow and develop inside and outside of the organization.

You can see from these factors that these are not women who necessarily want to leave their organizations. So, why do they walk out? Because as explored in Chapter 2, in the drive – conscious or otherwise – for the youthful, male, full-time-led organization, the ambitious qualities of these women are neither recognized, nor prized enough. So they walk away because: (a) they have to; and (b) they want to. Women want to fulfil these three ambitions, and if not with you, then with someone else – or on their own.

Enjoyment, flexibility, and growth – not a bad list if you are still wondering how to keep your midlife women!

Feeding all parts of my life

So, what many respondents are describing is not a decrease in ambition, but an increased recognition of how this ambition might be realized at this stage of their life. For example, success is realized through 'excitement not status' for Jude, 'ambition not aggression' for Donna, and 'stimulus, not scrambling my way up' for Nora. Money is important – often critical for many women with the later pension age – but not an end in itself, 'I've never done what I've done for money, I've done it for stability, I've done it to feel safe.' 'Agency and choice' are desired commodities. For many more respondents the language of achievement at midlife is about 'adventure... challenge... change... creativity... learning'. Meera describes the desire to 'feed all parts of my life' and Kathy suggests: 'I think women make a judgement call in favour of life rather than work more easily and with more conviction than a man would.'

This desire for a greater work/life balance is noteworthy, in that the more constrained the need to remain full-time within the organization, the more significance is attached to leaving. Indeed, the language used is more akin to escape than retirement. Kathy is 51, on the board of a financial institution and waiting for her pension to enjoy her '15 years of freedom', and describes a 'yearning, a longing, for fresh air and freedom'. The language Kathy uses is so evocative of flight. Nina describes shrugging off her 'restraints' whilst Kristin, in leaving her organization, has 'rid myself of the shackles'. Chris, in planning for her future, describes her 'escape route', 'I'm building, I'm starting to think about my lifeboat, rather than having my lifeboat thrust upon me.'

On the face of it, the data suggests the respondents intend to leave their roles with dreams that include being a school governor, a mindfulness/yoga teacher, a world traveller, an NED (non-executive director), or running a tea shop. Yet a closer look at the data demonstrates women who want to give so much more to their organization, but the company is too inflexible to allow it. Despite Kathy's strong language surrounding escape and freedom, she later discusses at length her desire to 'continue with pleasure', as receipt of her pension will give her options. She is clear that she intends to 'fill my life in the future as well, I don't want to just stop'. And as much as Cyn is emphatic about leaving the NHS on receipt of her pension, she has also just embarked on a part-time master's degree (which she studies for alongside her full-time nursing role and five children) just in case she 'changes her mind'. Chris is hoping her company will retain her well into her 60s and articulates her desire for flexibility, balanced by the aspiration to be appreciated and valued:

> I think there needs to be a conversation to be had which goes, 'how can we get the best out of you so it's a win/win for both of us?' You know, 'we love the way you do whatever you do, how can we get more of that?' 'How do we dial that up, dial down the other stuff that's getting in the way and negotiate a way that's going to work?' I would love them to say to me, 'Well, you're 60 Chris, we've loved you being here, you've had a great impact, is there any way you can work for three days a week?' I'd say yeah, terrific.

Min, 53, describes this well. She is on the board of her NHS Trust, and well aware that work is a major part of her identity:

> What I am, my persona, manifests itself in what I do. So, work is very important to me. It's not the be all and end all, but it is important to me and it's taken me till I'm 50 to realize that.

Min has no intention of giving up work, expressing an ambition to remain in work and step up further. But she is also articulate about her need to include learning as part of her motivation to achieve at work:

> *I want to keep learning. I think to make sure you don't feel like you've arrived, you've finished, that is the destination. Work itself is not a destination for me, it's a stop on the journey for whatever the rest of my life should be. Learning means doors open, and that gives me flexibility to say, you know, I'm a grown up now. I can make a choice about it.*

Creativity and adventure are words repeated throughout Kristin's interview. She describes her organization as offering just 'stifling sameness' and suggests:

> *It wasn't physical energy that I was lacking, quite the contrary, I had loads of energy and loads of ideas and loads of things I wanted to do, but it's just this stifling sameness that I just found really, really dull.*

Her energy and ambition are now being directed towards studying for a PhD.

What unites these stories is women saving their talent for a later time in their life when they can afford to realize it. Each woman has a different part of her life she wants to feed.

Full-time foolishness

However, the corporate requirement for leaders to be full-time remains implacable. As long as this remains the case, the ambition, energy, and desire of women like those described above remains untapped. There are very few examples within my study of women holding a leading role within their organization, whilst retaining the ability to operate part-time – unless (like Nora and Ana) they run the company. The male order has a firm grasp. Bel, a single woman and breadwinner, articulates her desire for a four-day working week, describing both a financial constraint as well as that of 'presenteeism' – the need to be a visible (virtual or otherwise), full-time presence:

> *This is a high energy job that I do, and which I've done against all odds with ME. Getting into my 50s makes me nervous. I have to work financially. It scares me, but I have to. So, I think if I could go part-time I could still do a really good job, but that's not accepted. You're seen then as on your way out, whereas I'm seeing it as a way of remaining on my way in.*

Similar to Bel, Chris' position is always influenced by her finances. Since her recent divorce, she is single and the breadwinner, and keen to stress her enjoyment of her role: 'I'm very happy here, it's a great role and there's a lot of opportunity, a lot of scope, from a people point of view.' Later in the interview Chris describes her anxiety at the pressure to retain her senior full-time position and build up a 'nest egg':

> *I'm fine now but have a lot of anxiety. I've got no safety nets in my life you know, I'm not going to inherit a palace in deepest darkest Sussex, my family are from Lincolnshire and have nothing. I've got nothing. There is no backup, there is no reserve.*

This is a generation of women who have witnessed unprecedented change in both pension rules (an increase in allowable pension age) and statutory retirement age – the latter of which was abolished in 2011.[1] I spoke to an equal number of women who had the luxury of financial freedom associated with home ownership and a final salary pension, as I did those who were financially struggling, particularly those who have seen their anticipated 'pension pot' deteriorate. There are women who have built up independent savings through their lives, and those who have lost most of their independent money through divorce. Gaynor discusses her resentment as her pension scheme at an academic institution has been 'wrecked', leaving her 'with no incentive to work here, other than I have to'. Robin provides a good example of someone who, at 62, is working full-time, has recently stepped up to the board – and has been the sole breadwinner for 21 years after her husband's chemical poisoning prevented him from working other than sporadically. She expresses how betrayed she feels by the government's 'goalpost' move:

> I thought I'd be able to finish at 60. What happened? Well the government happened! Some of my friends have retired at 60 because they work for organizations where you can take your pension at 60. But most women I know work for organizations who have moved their goalposts along with the government's pension plans.

Others are questioning the workplace culture itself. Meera's role in leading the agenda within her organization for diversity and inclusion has been described previously, and she is passionate about valuing difference, particularly related to the age agenda. She is equally thoughtful about the challenges of this, not only in terms of trying to get her agenda noticed and taken seriously within her organization, but also questioning the very culture she is endeavouring to change:

> I work really hard to get more women at senior levels in these organizations, but why would anyone want to be a senior member of these type of organizations? They're designed by men, and women wouldn't design them like this, the cultures, the structures, the politics. We wouldn't design these places, so why would we want to be part of

*them? I think that's a fundamental challenge with this
'Women on Boards' agenda. We need to try to change the
organization, not just try to squeeze more women into
this mould.*

What Meera is challenging is the structural and systemic
make-up of her organization – a patriarchal set-up that
plays to the freedom, ability and desire to work full-time,
where success is equated with the prioritizing of full-time
work above all other areas in life. She has been offered a
move across to the fee-earning part of the business, as long
as she works full-time, but is clear that she is not driven
by 'the long hours, lots of travel, uncontrolled lifestyle, so
I'm wary about stepping into something that takes control
away'. When I asked what other areas in her life Meera
would like to pay more attention to (if she wasn't working
full-time), I am given a list of her voluntary work within
the local primary school and university board; care for her
siblings and nieces; and increased visits with her parents
and in-laws who are in care. It is a rich list that is ambitious
in its own way, combining paid work, voluntary work,
care, friends, and family. Unfortunately, despite her senior
position, Meera feels unable to tackle the organization's
systemic set-up. She discussed leaving and placing her
wide-ranging energies elsewhere.

Meera's practical recognition of the need for systemic change
is echoed by the leadership scholar, Professor Amanda
Sinclair, who suggests:

*Women often don't feel themselves to be powerful, and
that is not just a matter of individual perception – it is
systemic property. Over generations and across cultures,
political and social systems have been constructed to
ensure women don't get access to power.*[2]

Being a change advocate

The language of revolt is central to this book because it is only through revolting that women can fully survive both the patriarchal set-up of the workplace and the mythology that writes middle-aged women off as, in Lisa Appignanesi's words, 'mad, bad and sad'.[3]

Within her organization, Lori, a 50-year-old talent director, is one example of what she calls a 'change advocate', using her voice and actions to demonstrate that job-sharing is possible at a senior level. Now a role model within her global organization and lobbying for international change, she expands on the possibility of greater flexibility for older women being considered in Latin America and Asia:

> *I had lots of messages, 'fantastic you've been able to make this happen', 'good on you', 'brilliant, we've been able to keep both of you'. So lots of credit for being able to make it happen. Even from our other global colleagues this is culturally really different, it's a first. Doing a job share was really quite alien to them, so they went, 'wow! how can we do this?' Even now they're working through their policies of how they could physically and legislatively make it happen again in the UK, Latin America and in Asia. Change is happening. I know it's slow, but at least it is starting.*

And women are often 'change advocates' for each other. I've always questioned the research that suggests female leaders are deliberately unhelpful to each other, or to other women in their organization. It is simply not my personal experience, or that of my clients, friends, and colleagues. Of course, you will be able to cite examples that run contrary to this, but in the main, women show up with generosity, assistance, and inspiration to each other. Within my study too, multiple examples were offered of proactive support and encouragement. There was a real sense of bringing women through, and a recognition of 'standing on the shoulders of giants' for those women who had already broken the glass ceiling. Min, 53, is passionate about using her position of influence on the board to develop women across her organization at all levels through coaching and mentoring:

The hard bit for many women is having the mentors, the sponsors, the people who give you the coaching, the determination and fan the flames a bit. So I am conscious of my responsibility as a female director to say, actually we should be promoting women, we should be working with women in a different way and using the skills they've got. If you want a career you've got to do your bit too as well, you're not going to get automatically promoted, it's a give and take, but I would champion the cause for women as long as there's breath in my body.

The importance of role models within an organization has been well noted by organizational scholars, and Sandra is a great example of this. As one of the oldest female executives in the media industry, who has faced considerable discrimination in her career and actively fought to bring this to public notice, she is aware of the positivity of remaining in her position:

There are so many young women saying, 'I admire you because you're an older woman, you're a real role model for me, you're a real example to people in the industry'. From younger people I felt a genuine respect and admiration for what I had learned, and I still feel that. Every year I do something at work that I've never done before, but I also help people to do something that I have done before, and I help them do it better, so they can learn by the failures and successes of the past.

Paula, 58, is a scientist within a government-funded organization. Her company breaks the normal organizational mould in many ways and perhaps comes closest to an example of cultural change advocacy. It is staffed at senior levels by older women (between 40 and 65, with one male exception), with flexibility built into the set-up:

> *So we have got all sorts of arrangements. People are running several roles usually, and it is probably the norm that people are working part-time, and they are either doing a different role, or hobby, or volunteering, the rest of the week or have caring responsibilities. You just lead from a position of what people feel comfortable with.*

What felt unusual in this interview is that Paula didn't present this as a radical organization, but just a normal, so-called, 'mix and match' place. The influence and role modelling of the female managing director is clear, as she actively seeks older people with interesting skill sets and networks to join the organization. Paula was clear about what kept this team productive:

> *Autonomy, flexibility and reducing bureaucracy is critical but, you know, the organization is about innovation and doing new things, so having that approach is helpful. People can suggest stuff and develop things and see where you get to. The notion that older people are not innovative is just a generalization and I don't do generalizations. You can meet people of 22 who have got that mentality, so it is not an age-related issue.*

What Paula's organization shows is that success can be reconfigured with a different approach to structure, to age, and to flexible working. Another person challenging ideas of leadership and advocating for change is Niamh. Niamh studied the notion of 'co-headship' for her master's, which is an attempt to bring women to the top of the profession and share skill sets in a participative manner. She describes how 'the Napoleonic head is a thing of the past' with schools recognizing that 'one person cannot embody all the features and functions' of the massive role of leading a school.

Meg, 57, a journalist and actor, provides an interesting example of reconfiguring success in the acting profession, as she consciously strives to work against the norm of the notoriously youth-oriented acting profession. Whether discussing menopause, acting or midlife, Meg is passionate about controlling her life through managing her mindset:

> *Filming seems to be more lucrative and I've been having more jobs filming. I'm now of the age where I get cast as the grandmother (laughs). I don't like going to the auditions and hearing they are looking for a grandmother, 'Oh god, great', but the roles are more interesting. Like any woman, the older you get, the more complex life is, and it's the same with acting. The roles are fuller, more in depth, more interesting, more complex. So, yes, I would like to make it expand. I'd like to play on it. I'd like to sell myself as an older woman. If that's what it takes, it's cool.*

The free-range woman!

Leaving an organization (loudly and visibly) is an active, vocal step towards change, rather than one of failure or 'opting out'. What scientists call 'individual entrepreneurialism' means to most of us leaving and setting up your own business, and there is an exponential increase in women at midlife transitioning to self-employment and female entrepreneurship.[4] Female entrepreneurs contribute some £85 billion to the UK economy, and according to Dame Alison Rose's (Chief Executive of NatWest Bank) 2022 government report,[5] if women were enabled to succeed at their own businesses at the same rate as men, their contribution to the UK economy would rise to £250 billion. The over-50s account for one in six of all new businesses starting up in the UK and are known as 'olderpreneurs' or 'silver start-ups'. Dismal terminology, but their hit rates are impressive – older people tend to have a 70% chance of making it through the first five years, as opposed to 28% of younger entrepreneurs.[6] And the trend of older women starting up businesses continues to rise, with women citing as reasons, energy, lack of guilt, amazing contacts, knowledge, and experience.[7] I love the story of Cherry Harker, who launched her swimwear business ZwimZuit in 2016 at the age of 76. She says,

> It seemed like the perfect time. I married when I was 30, spent my 30s and 40s focused on family life, supporting my husband in his business. I battled breast cancer in my 50s, cervical cancer in my 60s, so now I finally had time to do something just for me. I don't see my age as a barrier.[8]

Women bring a different life experience to business – one that needs to be recognized more positively. Research carried out for a report called 'Older Female Entrepreneurship' by Isabella Moore, a former chair of the Women's Enterprise Panel, hints at this in its finding that, 'a positive proactive attitude to developing a business activity may be based on older women reassessing their lives. The need to achieve recognition, status and a sense of achievement is the motive for entrepreneurship.'[9]

On the flipside, it's worth noting that many women are 'reluctant entrepreneurs'. That is, running their own business is a necessity, a constrained choice, because the more conventional, secure path of corporate employment is blocked for all the reasons we've discussed in this book, be it discrimination or dissatisfaction, lack of flexibility, or recognition. Ana is a great example here. Now leading a successful small legal firm, she left her employers after their demand for her full-time attendance on promotion to equity partner:

> *I asked why? And they said, 'well, to prove your commitment'. I reminded them they can get hold of me any time day or night, that I bill more than anyone else in the firm despite working three days to their five days, and that I'd be unhappy and unproductive. They didn't agree, so I quit and set up my own business. Now flexible working is built into my business for everyone. It's integral to our values and way of working.*

Nora, too, describes the 'insanity' of working full-time within the existing organizational confines, whilst Ines is clear that:

> *women over 50 are much less willing to pretend that they are going to tap dance enthusiastically for the new broom that is constantly arising. You think (groans) enough of the new brooms, I have already seen five new brooms.*

Nora describes the patriarchal culture as 'men trying to carry on through the corporate ladders and still believing they've got somewhere to go'. As a serial entrepreneur, who has just sold her business for several million and is currently setting up several new companies with women deliberately at the helm, Nora is clear about her priorities:

> *I'm certainly competitive and like to win and all of those things, but I don't think I've got all consuming ambition, and I wonder if a lot of older women don't have all consuming ambition? In the end all the corny bits really matter. You've got to have your family. I suspect a lot of women when they balance their values think, 'actually if there was a problem over here with the family I'd give up all of this [her career]'.*

Nora is cognizant that the money she has made gives her choices, and when one listens to her interview (and I remember the sensation sitting with her), you are infused with her passion for business, for life, for growth and creativity:

> In every business I lead, I'm very concerned to bring up the next generation, build successes behind them, be generous with knowledge and nurture their talent. I love a project, but most of all, I love helping other people be happy in their work.

As she is currently investing in three further businesses, including how we experience bingo in the 21st century, Nora discusses 'retiring' somewhere around her 80th birthday.

Nora's proactive, positive nature is a good place to end this chapter, the purpose of which is to highlight change that is happening. I wish I had a library full of extensive radical examples and broader solutions of reconfigured success, but the reality is the pace of change for gender equality remains glacial, despite some beautiful role models. Key to this third part of the book is the recognition that ambition, and the language of achievement, plays a significant role in the life of the professional female at, and beyond, midlife. Far from a desire to abandon the corporate game, the findings highlight a majority of respondents interested and engaged in their careers, and willing to push through considerable hurdles to achieve their career goals. For many, this is enabled after a tumultuous midlife period of loss and adversity has abated, or been accepted, freeing their sharp minds towards a new chapter of growth and accomplishment.

The desire to combine this ambition with flexibility is keen, with many respondents describing the sensation of feeling 'time poor, not age poor'. For some respondents a flexible work/life balance is financially viable, whilst others are constrained to work full-time. The frustration and anger with the existing set-up of the patriarchal organization is palpable, with the lack of flexibility described by many women as a 'tragedy', or 'outrage'. But respondents continued to find new ways to reject the decline narrative laid out for them, and revolt against existing 'norms', offering fragments of hope for a reconfiguration of what success can mean for a professional female at midlife.

CONCLUSION

A POSITIVE AGENDA FOR CHANGE

Haply a woman's voice may do some good.
(William Shakespeare, *Henry V*)

Where are all the female leaders?

Well, probably not in your business! With women leaving their companies at the highest rate ever seen in corporate America, Europe, and the UK, they are voting with their feet and revolting against the status quo.[1] This is the so-called 'Great Breakup', that is, women are demanding more from work and leaving their companies in unprecedented numbers to get it. As the authors of the McKinsey report, 'Women in the Workplace', state:

> *Women are already significantly underrepresented in leadership. For years, fewer women have risen through the ranks because of the 'broken rung' at the first step up to management. Now, companies are struggling to hold onto the relatively few women leaders they have. And all of these dynamics are even more pronounced for women of colour.*[2]

Why is this the case? As I've recounted in this book, women are struggling to turn the tide of the unchanging power dynamic; they are often unable or unwilling to work full-time as they experience a collision of midlife events, and because they actively choose to place their energy and ambition elsewhere. Usually under their control. *That is, middle-aged women break up with their companies either because they have to, or they want to.* And the impact of this has yet to be accounted for. But what is known is that once older women depart from leadership roles, a vicious cycle follows.[3] Not only does experience, wisdom, and talent drain from the company, but younger women lose their role models and follow suit, and male leadership ossifies at the top. And how has this been allowed to continue? I can think of at least three reasons: female attrition is ignored with lip service paid to the retention and promotion of older women; unpaid care is expected from women at all stages of their career; and gendered ageism is excluded from the diversity agenda.

And it is an exclusion. In the main, studies reporting on the state of women in the workplace consider their marginalization from the perspectives of race, disability, sexuality, and gender identity. But age is rarely part of the conversation (even though once any of these characteristics are intersected with age, the women have an even harder time to be promoted in the workplace). What this means is that the exclusion of gendered ageism from the diversity dialogue enables lazy assumptions to perpetuate and hides the systemic reasons behind the decision of each middle-aged woman who leaves her organization.

And just to briefly recap on five of the most prevalent assumptions that inhibit progress:

There's no problem: A single statistic puts the scale of the problem in perspective: according to the largest study of the state of women in corporate America, 'Women in the Workplace' (2022), for every woman at director level who gets promoted to the next level, two women directors leave their company.[4] And there's more. In the UK, women might be showing up at board level in non-executive director roles, but the percentage of women at executive (and crucially, employed) level has flatlined at 13% for FTSE 100 companies, and 11% for FTSE 250 companies – with only 47 women holding these roles in 45 companies. Only two companies have two women in executive roles. Again, flying under the radar is the issue of age, with the average age of the female in an executive role being 51 years.[5]

They don't fit: OK, it's true. But it's hard to 'fit' when you are in the minority. Remember Jude's struggle in Chapter 5 not being able to share her menopause symptoms with her all-male colleagues, or Chris and Meera in Chapter 1 unable to recall a single other senior woman of their age in their organization. There is enough understanding now that there need to be at least three women in a team for their voices to be heard.[6] This is not an individual problem of 'fitting in'. This is a systemic question of diversity, inclusion, and belonging – whether at management, leadership, or board level. Women don't fit because the system has been built to not accommodate them; it is not women who don't fit, it is that the system has been built to fit another kind of life from the one they live.

They don't want it: I feel like I'm in a pantomime when I go, 'Oh yes, they do'! But women *do* want to progress. At the risk of repetition, 70% of the women within my study wanted to step up in their careers, were clear in their enjoyment and innate interest in work and possessed a desire to grow and develop inside and outside of the organization. But midlife women don't want to feed their ambition at the expense of a sustainable work/life balance. They want to reconstrue their lives to achieve in a different way and are desiring, demanding, and needing flexibility to achieve their goals.

They can't cope: This is just dull discrimination. Show me a middle-aged woman and I'll guarantee you a woman with extraordinary resilience, who has learned through her adult life to juggle her career, caring duties, health concerns, friendships, and family. She may face temporary setbacks, but they are transitory, and women come back stronger and more able to face the next chapter.

They are not available: I would politely suggest that anyone who says this is looking in the wrong place, using the wrong search consultants, or expecting a résumé that looks like the typical, linear-careered, male CV. Many middle-aged women have résumés with breaks, hiccups, and different turns, which, I would argue, only makes the midlife woman a more interesting and worthwhile candidate. Yes, women need to learn to 'sell' their so-called squiggly careers more effectively, but companies equally need to value the richness of a life well lived.

Ten provocations for change

The dynamics of discrimination are subtle and well embedded. This means that when discrimination becomes habitual, exclusionary practices are not noticed or commented on and frequently invisible – just not noticed. For change to happen and to have an organizational impact, it will require the desire to *choose* to notice. And a number of societal shifts may compel you to increase your awareness. This includes the global decrease in birth rates and increase of the ageing population; the slow realization of equality and inclusion; and governmental policy and societal shifts acting against discriminatory practices – as well as employees and customers, who are demanding equality, support, and fairness in its many diverse forms.

There is plenty of evidence in this book and beyond that suggests professional older women have the will and energy, the mental capacity, and the ambition to further achieve. Moreover, despite manifold and complex experiences of loss and exclusion at this time of life for so many women I interviewed, midlife impels a period of ambition, positivity, and growth.

So if you are an interested stakeholder in business, perhaps in human resources, with a responsibility for diversity and inclusion, or a senior leader, here are ten provocations (and a bank of questions) to set you on your journey towards change:

1. **Are you prepared to take this seriously?** There is lip service and there is action. If you want to make a start, look at who has responsibility for ED&I (Equality, Diversity, and Inclusion) in your organization. Here are four big questions to help you get started:

   • What is the reporting mechanism and how do you hold leadership to account?
   • How are the ED&I goals integrated into business strategy, succession planning, and leadership competencies?
   • How public is your leadership in promoting (and role-modelling) ED&I practices?
   • In what ways could you publicize visible targets for improvement, including a 'here's how we are doing' message? Now there's direct action!

2. **Where is your problem?** Look at the make-up of your company. Draw up some visual statistics of women at every level. Pie chart, bar chart, line graph, it doesn't matter, but visualizing the issue is really helpful for everyone to understand exactly what is happening, at what level and where. Then take a closer look and think about the following:

   • What is your female pipeline and where does it start to 'leak'? (What I mean by 'leaking' is at what point do women leave the organization?)

- How many women are in management, executive, and senior leadership roles (compared to men)?
- How do these numbers shift as you get higher up the organization?
- How has the data changed since Covid-19 (which has disproportionately affected women's career progression)?
- Find out why midlife women are leaving your company through confidential exit interviews, and what would enable them to stay.

And if you know you are holding back because of a lack of data, don't let this be an excuse for inaction. Anywhere you start will be a positive!

3. **What does your age data look like?** Now add in age data to your chart above. Explore the impact of age at every level of your organization, as it's common for companies to invest in older workers at lower levels, whilst ignoring their departure at senior levels. How does it shift your understanding of the gender issues around the organization? Choose to notice what is going on with women post-45 years in your company. What are their promotion, retention, and attrition rates? Where do discriminatory practices hinder their progression? (For example, how many women are leaving at menopausal age?)

Whilst you're exploring age data, look at the ways that 'age' is mentioned and measured (or missed out) in your diversity reporting. Is it one of the diversity reporting segments? What assumptions are being made about your older workers (e.g. it's all about retirement)?

4. **How about conducting midlife check-ins?** I cannot recommend this more highly. And I can immediately think of many women whose decisions to exit their

company could have been stalled with a very good, careful, internal conversation. Your midlife executives are people you have invested in through their careers and, ideally, you do not want to lose them. Often their resignations can come as a surprise as you had little idea of the ways in which they were struggling/juggling. Or perhaps they are simply in the process of reflecting on the next chapter of their lives, and the full-on, full-time life you are offering is not good enough. Sometimes it is just a case of a lack of appreciation. As you've read in this book, lives at this stage become challenging in a very different way from staff at a younger age, and it is worth your investment to find out how they are doing and where their career aspirations lie. To get this right:

- Ensure you are not singling out any one woman. Or perhaps conduct midlife check-ins across your male/female population.
- Ensure your intent is sincere and positive. The point of a check-in is care, curiosity, and appreciation. It goes without saying it is confidential.
- A good check-in is a genuine attempt to understand what is going on in the life of the woman in front of you, not always personal, but definitely professional.
  - What is their career aspiration for the next chapter of their lives, and how can you help them realize it?
  - What will motivate them to take this next step?
  - What might stop them from doing this?

5. **How flexible are you?** I know this is not new, I know you have been wrestling with this for years and hybrid working has only accelerated the conversation. Yet in the reconstruction of what success looks like to this age group, data from my study shows that flexibility is of overriding concern, with midlife women facing

multifarious generational caring demands. As caring responsibilities for elderly parents in particular are only going to increase with our ageing population, this is an urgent, contemporary debate. Flexible working, or more recently the experiment of the four-day week, appears to be easier to imagine or put into practice at lower levels in an organization. Women consistently report having to work full-time once they reach senior level, with limited access to job-sharing at this level. With flexibility, caring responsibilities are realized in tandem with the desire to achieve. Without flexibility, older women leave organizations silently or realize 'revolt' elsewhere, forging careers in different forms.

6. **Is your senior leadership team stuck in the past?** This is probably the trickiest point of all as it will require you to ask those at the top of your organization to take a good look at themselves, their structure, their policies – and their willingness to change! Perhaps the structure of your leadership team, of your executive committees, needs reimagining to enable flexible working, temporary leave, or even role changing? If you know there's the sense of 'this is how we do it here', you're stuck in the past!

Also perhaps the executive roles are stale, stifling the possibility for creativity? If you remember, what women said they wanted was the opportunity to grow and develop. It's worth remembering the three points I made at the beginning of Chapter 10 – that is, to stay in an organization midlife women want enjoyment, flexibility, and growth. It's not all about time away from the organization, everyone wants to feel their time 'in' is meaningful and, dare I say it, fun. Lead a future-imagining exercise with your senior leadership team – I've always found it useful to go to an extreme first in order to scale back to a more realistic point. Here are some questions to whet your appetite:

- Imagine this senior leadership team all worked part-time, what would that be like/feel like?
- What could be the unrealized benefits from this?
- Imagine you all swap job roles (in a controlled way!), for six months. What would everyone learn? How would that be useful?
- Imagine you are allowed to grow in an entirely new direction within the organization, where would you go and what would you do?
- If you were to job-share your role, giving you more time and space outside of work, what would you use that time and space to do?
- What is the most radical thing this team could do to breathe new life into the way you work?
- What is the smallest thing you could do that would make the biggest difference?

Make this conversation as safe and as playful as possible and see where you land and what opportunities arise from the conversation to shift the strictures of your senior teams.

7. **How do you seek out, leverage, value, and hear different voices?** If you have a responsibility for diversity or leadership, it is really useful to sit in on a range of management and leadership meetings and listen to the share of voice. Which teams excel at share of voice and what do they do differently? Seek out meetings where women are in the minority. In what ways are their voices heard? In what ways are their voices excluded? How can you ensure women feel psychologically safe to speak up and have their voices heard alongside their male colleagues?

8. **What training is provided at midlife and beyond for women?** Given that the data shows women are interested in growth and mastery as they age, is your training directed solely towards them stepping down

or out – or directed towards women stepping up and growing with you? In what ways are you stimulating their imagination and creativity to stay and grow with you?

9. **How do you sponsor the career progression of your midlife women?** As men have greater access to well-honed formal and informal networks, women need greater sponsorship through your organization in order to get to the top – whether by men or women. Wherever the power sits, is where the sponsor should come from.

10. **How menopause-friendly is your organization?** That some organizations are managing to break the silence over the menopause is noteworthy. How are you supporting women going through menopause transition? What is your menopause policy and how is this being distributed, discussed, and visualized? Don't let your menopause policy be a tick-box exercise, or something that's stuck in a file and ignored. Far better to act, and this doesn't need to be a cost- or resource-heavy exercise. For example, companies who have championed best practice give the following examples of initiatives:

- Clear leadership by creating a supportive environment that de-stigmatizes the topic. Refer to menopause at an employee event, at onboarding or the induction process. Make it clear your organization recognizes menopause and is prepared to help with it.
- Train menopause advocates to drive awareness and education.
- Hold weekly lunch-and-learn sessions open to all colleagues covering a wide range of menopause topics (including menopause for men).
- Launch a menopause page on employee well-being hubs; provide books or resources on your intranet.

- Offer practical tools, e.g. a template GP letter.
- Redesign your uniform if appropriate to ensure it is made out of breathable material.
- Simplify policies, e.g. making it easier to order a fan at work.
- Work with an external provider for independent and confidential information, e.g. BUPA, who provide a menopause healthline.

But there isn't a 'one size fits all' approach, and evidence consistently points to the value to midlife women of receiving confidential, tailored, and specialist advice at work about their transition-related symptoms.

What is most important is that you listen, recognize, and highlight the diversity of experience of your employed midlife women. If you are going to design policies, guidance, training, start from a position of listening to women's lived experience and incorporating their recommendations that will be right for your company. Or to summarize the above in fewer than seven words (which would have made a much shorter book):

Find out, show it matters, act.

And what can the middle-aged woman take from this?

For women who are revolting

My heartfelt wish is that women reading this book recognize their own experience in these pages – not that I'm wishing discrimination or midlife collision on anyone! But if you have felt the weight of discrimination on your shoulders, unable to see a way through the existing power structure, you are not alone. If you feel embattled with midlife collisions, whether that be menopause, caring challenges, anxiety for your children's welfare, concern for your future, or just a messy chaos of all of these, other women are in the same boat.

But you will, and do, come through this time. As the fabulous Eleanor Mills, founder of Noon, the social media platform for women at midlife, suggests, hard-won wisdom forged from fire gives women confidence and solidity in their lives once through that fire. These are her so-called 'Queenagers' – terminology with a nice element of revolution that appeals to me![7] This is the time women become fed up with the existing status quo of their organization and want to reconstruct their career on their terms. There are plenty of women like you doing exactly this.

What is critical is that you understand how important you are in changing the system. Once women exit the system quietly, nothing changes. Good women are leaving companies silently. So instead, shout, roar, and bang the drums. Revolt! And what does revolution look like?

- Be visible and vocal. Be a role model for younger women. Let them see you stepping up; let them see your vulnerability; let them see the whole person at work and know that's OK.
- Challenge banter and assumptions. Don't let people get away with circulating old-fashioned myths about women or older women. You are not 'turning off' at midlife, nor do you necessarily want to retire. You don't want your mother's midlife or to be defined by the menopause or your reproductive body.
- You do not need fixing, the system does. For every individual issue that is labelled as a woman's problem, there is a systemic reason behind it. For example, confidence. Commonly, women don't lack confidence in themselves, they lack confidence that the company will change sufficiently for their voices to be heard. Talk system, not individual.

- Advocate for women: for succession planning, for promotion, and retention. Help women within your own company rise up. Be their sponsor, their mentor, their friend. Join together and make communal waves.
- If you are in menopause transition and struggling, please get help. You do not have to struggle, to 'live with it', or just be satisfied with anti-depressants. If your GP practice has no specialized help, look at the British Menopause Society site for a list of specialist practitioners, and there you will find someone who will listen to you.
- If you are considering leaving your organization, talk to HR about what would make you stay. Encourage your organization to consider changes they could make that would have made you reconsider your decision. What would help the next woman?

The novelist, Isabel Allende, in her TED talk, 'How to live passionately – no matter your age', said, 'Inside, I feel good, I feel charming, seductive, sexy. Nobody else sees this.'[8] I see it. I see the worth of the vibrant and creative middle-aged woman, who adds immeasurable energy, productivity, and wisdom to the organization. And I'm cautiously optimistic that society is learning to see it too and to recognize the beautiful reality of the value of the middle-aged woman.

NOTES

Introduction

[1] Krivkovich, A., et al. (2022) 'Women in the Workplace'. Download report at: www.mckinsey.com/featured-insights/diversity-and-inclusion/women-in-the-workplace

[2] Some examples: Trethewey, A. (2001) 'Reproducing and resisting the master narrative of decline: midlife professional women's experiences of aging', *Management Communication Quarterly*, 15 (2), 183–226.

Mitchell, B. A., and Lovegreen, L. D. (2009) 'The empty nest syndrome in midlife families: a multimethod exploration of parental gender differences and cultural dynamics', *Journal of Family Issues*, 30 (12), 1651–1650.

Muhlbauer, V. (2007) 'The well-being and quality of life of women over 50: a gendered-age perspective'. In Muhlbauer, V. and Chrisler, J. C. (eds), *Women over 50: psychological perspectives*. New York: Springer, pp. 95–111.

Wray, S. (2007) 'Women making sense of midlife: ethnic and cultural diversity', *Journal of Aging Studies*, 21, 31–42.

[3] O'Neil, D., and Bilimoria, D. (2005) 'Women's career development phases: idealism, endurance and reinvention', *Career Development International*, 10 (3), 168–189.

Pringle, J. K., and Dixon, K. M. (2003) 'Reincarnating life in the careers of women', *Career Development International*, 8 (6), 291–300.

[4] Lord Davies Review (2011) 'Women on Boards'. Available from: https//assets.publishing.gov.uk.

Hampton-Alexander Review (2021) 'Improving gender balance – a 5 year summary report'. Download report at: https://ftsewomenleaders.com/wp-content/uploads/2021/02/HA-REPORT-2021_FINAL.pdf

[5] Hampton-Alexander Review (2018) 'FTSE women leaders: improving gender balance in FTSE leadership'. Download report at: https://ftsewomenleaders.com/wp-content/uploads/2018/11/HA-Review-Report-2018.pdf

[6] Mills, E. (2021) 'A woman's life doesn't end at 40 – so why does society make us feel that way?', *The Guardian*, 13 March.

[7] Sarner, M. (2017) 'Meet the women launching startups in their 50s', *The Guardian*, 28 August.

8 Federation of Small Business (2022) 'Supporting women's enterprise in the UK: the economic case'. Download report at: www.fsb.org.uk/resource-report/supporting-women-s-enterprise-in-the-uk.html

9 Government Office for Science (2022) 'Future of an ageing population'. Download report at: https://assets.publishing.service.gov.uk/government/uploads/system/uploads/attachment_data/file/816458/future-of-an-ageing-population.pdf

10 Learning & Work Institute (2019) 'Local skills and deficits and spare capacity'. Download report at: www.local.gov.uk/sites/default/files/documents/FINAL%20LGA%202019%20Skills%20Gaps%20report%20final%20December%202019.pdf

11 Power, K. (2020) 'The COVID-19 pandemic has increased the care burden of women and families', *Sustainability: Science, Practice and Policy*, 16 (1), 67–73. DOI: 10.1080/15487733.2020.1776561

House of Commons Women & Equality Committee (2021) 'Unequal impact? Coronavirus and the gendered economic impact'. Download report at: https://committees.parliament.uk/publications/4597/documents/46478/default/

12 Here are some examples: Vinnicombe, S. & Tessaro, M. (2022) 'The Female FTSE Report, What works?' Cranfield School of Management. Download report at: www.cranfield.ac.uk/femaleftseboardreport

Desvaux, G., et al. (2017) *Women matter: ten years of insights on gender diversity*. New York: McKinsey & Co.

Goldman Sachs Portfolio Strategy (2020) 'Womenomics: Europe moving ahead'. Download report at: www.goldmansachs.com/insights/pages/gs-research/womenomics-europe-moving-ahead/report.pdf

Hersh, E. (2016) 'Why diversity matters'. Download report at: www.hsph.harvard.edu/ecpe/why-diversity-matters-women-on-boards-of-directors/

House of Commons Library (2022) 'Women and the UK economy'. Download report at: https://commonslibrary.parliament.uk/research-briefings/sn06838/

Roffey Park (2022) 'Female leadership in the workplace'. Available from: www.roffeypark.ac.uk/knowledge-and-learning-resources-hub/female-lworkplace-building-a-workplace-culture-of-gender-balance-and-inclusivity/

Topping, A. (2022) 'Companies with female leaders outperform those dominated by men, data shows', www.theguardian.com, 6 March.

13 Devillard, S., Hunt, V., and Yee, L. (2018) 'Still looking for room at the top: ten years of research on women in the workplace'. Download report at: www.mckinsey.com/featured-insights/gender-equality/

still-looking-for-room-at-the-top-ten-years-of-research-on-women-in-the-workplace

14 Green, M., Peters, R., and Young, J. (2020) 'People profession 2030: a collective view of future trends', Chartered Institute of People Development (CIPD).

Chapter 1: Problem, what problem?

1 Whittington-Hill, L. (2022) 'Pop culture's problem with middle-aged women', www.catapult.co, 28 July.

2 Darnell, D., and Gadiesh, O. (2013) *Gender equality in the UK: the next stage of the journey.* Boston: Bain & Co.

3 Broadbridge, A., and Simpson, R. (2011) '25 years on, reflecting on the past and looking to the future in gender and management research', *British Journal of Management*, 22 (3), 470–483.

4 Catalyst (2022) 'Women in management'. Available from: www.catalyst.org/research/women-in-management

5 Marren, C., and Bazeley, A. (2022) 'Sex and Power 2022', The Fawcett Society. Available from: www.fawcettsociety.org.uk/sex-power-2022

6 Official Monetary and Financial Institutions Forum (OMFIF) (2022) 'Gender Balance Index'. Available from: www.omfif.org/gbi22

7 Office for Economic Cooperation and Development (OECD) (2021) 'Gender equality'. Available from: www.oecd.org/gender/data/women-in-senior-management-roles-at-energy-firms-remains-stubbornly-low-but-efforts-to-improve-gender-diversity-are-moving-apace.htm

8 Cohen, A. (2020) 'What is a Peter problem'? Jaw dropping study of UK CEOs reveals more named Peter than women', www.fastcompany.com, 29 July.

9 Goodwin, K. (2021) 'Revealing the facts and figures of London's statues and monuments', www.artuk.org, 21 October.

10 McKinsey & Co/Lean In (2021) 'Women in the Workplace'. Download report at: www.mckinsey.com/~/media/mckinsey/featured%20insights/diversity%20and%20inclusion/women%20in%20the%20workplace%202021/women-in-the-workplace-2021.pdf

11 Ibid.

12 Vinnicombe, S., and Tessaro, M. (2022) 'The Female FTSE Report, What works?' Cranfield School of Management. Download report at: www.cranfield.ac.uk/femaleftseboardreport

13 Marren and Bazeley, 'Sex and Power 2022', p. 2.

[14] McGraw, M. (2022) 'What it takes to be an age-friendly workplace', www.worldatwork.org, 27 September.

[15] Diligent Institute (2021) 'Global boardroom diversity trends and updates'. Download report at: www.diligentinstitute.com/commentary/global-boardroom-diversity-trends-and-updates-from-the-diligent-institute/

[16] Catalyst, 'Women in management'.

[17] Workplace Gender Equality Agency, www.wgea.gov.au

[18] Mercer (2020) 'Let's get real about equality'. Available from: www.mercer.com/our-thinking/next-generation-global-research-when-women-thrive-2020.html

[19] Eurostat (2021) 'Women remain outnumbered in management'. Available from: https://ec.europa.eu/eurostat/web/products-eurostat-news/-/edn-20210305-2

[20] World Economic Forum (2021) 'It will take another 136 years to close the gender gap'. Available from: www.weforum.org/agenda/2021/04/136-years-is-the-estimated-journey-time-to-gender-equality/

[21] Cranfield University press report (2021) 'A tale of two halves, Cranfield University publishes its 2021 Female FTSE Board Report', Cranfield University, 7 October, p. 1.

[22] Hampton-Alexander Review (2018) 'FTSE women leaders: improving gender balance in FTSE leadership'. Available from: https://ftsewomenleaders.com/wp-content/uploads/2018/11/HA-Review-Report-2018.pdf

[23] Ibid., p. 7.

[24] Osborne, S. (2018) 'Pitiful and patronising excuses for lack of women in FTSE boardrooms revealed', wwwtheindependent.co.uk, 31 May.

[25] Konrad, A., and Erkust, S. (2008) 'Critical mass. The impact of three of more women on corporate boards', Organizational Dynamics, 37 (20), 145–164.

[26] Legal summaries such as: Silverstein, R. (2022) 'Hung out to dry', Browne Jacobson, www.brownejacobson.com/insights/hung-out-to-dry

[27] Höpfl, H., and Matilal, S. (2007) 'The lady vanishes: some thoughts on women and leadership', Journal of Organizational Change Management, 20 (2), 198–208

[28] Levy, B. R. (2009) 'Stereotype embodiment: a psychosocial approach to aging', Current Directions in Psychological Science, 18, 332–336. DOI: 10.1111=j.1467- 8721.2009.01662.x

[29] Evans, M. (2017) *The persistence of gender inequality*. Cambridge, UK: Polity Press.

Chapter 2: Ageing in the workplace

[1] Fineman, S. (2011) *Organizing age*. Oxford: Oxford University Press.

[2] Marcus, B. (2021) 'Gendered ageism affects women's job security and financial viability', www.forbes.com, 20 September.

[3] For example: Reuters.com (2023) 'Britain needs you: Hunt urges older people to rejoin the workforce'. Available from: www.reuters.com/world/uk/britain-needs-you-hunt-urges-older-people-rejoin-workforce

Smith, J. (2022) 'Over 50s urged to return to work to deal with staff shortages'. Available from: https://workplaceinsight.net/over-50s-urged-to-return-to-work-to-deal-with-staff-shortages

[4] Irving, P. (2018) 'When no one retires'. In Irving, P., 'The ageing workforce', *Harvard Business Review*, November, 3–8.

Calo, T. J. (2008) 'Talent management in the era of the aging workforce: the critical role of knowledge transfer', *Public Personnel Management*, 37 (4), 403–416.

Strack, R., Baier, J., and Fahlander, A. (2008) 'Managing demographic risk', *Harvard Business Review*, February, 119–128.

[5] Byrne, D. (2023) 'Sorry, Jeremy Hunt, we older people want to work. But bosses just don't want us to'. Available from: www.theguardian.com/commentisfree/2023/feb/01/jeremy-hunt-older-people-work-bosses-just-dont-want-us-to

[6] Fineman, *Organizing age*, p. 58.

[7] Gullette, M. M. (1997) *Declining to decline: cultural combat and the politics of midlife*. University Press of Virginia.

Gullette, M. M. (2004) *Aged by culture*. Chicago: University of Chicago Press.

[8] Jaques, E. (1965) 'Death and the midlife crisis', *The International Journal of Psycho-Analysis*, 46 (4), 502–514, 406.

[9] Druckerman, P. (2018) 'How the midlife crisis came to be'. Read full article here: www.theatlantic.com/family/archive/2018/05/the-invention-of-the-midlife-crisis/561203

[10] MIDUS study: Brim, O. G., Ryff, C. D., and Kessler, R. C. (2005) 'Studies on successful midlife development', in Brim, O. G., Ryff, C. D., and Kessler, R. C. (eds), *How healthy are we? A national study of well-being at midlife*. Chicago: University of Chicago Press, pp. 1–34.

[11] The term 'gendered ageism' was first coined by two scholars, Catherine Itzen and Christopher Phillipson, in 1995 in a paper called, 'Gendered ageism: a double jeopardy for women', in Itzen and Janet Newman's book, *Gender, culture and organizational change*. Routledge. It was later popularized in media reports in the 2020s.

[12] Perez, C. C. (2020) *Invisible women: data biases in a world designed for men*. London: Vintage.

[13] AARP (2022) 'Age discrimination among workers aged 50-plus'. Download report at: www.aarp.org/research/topics/economics/info-2022/workforce-trends-older-adults-age-discrimination.html

[14] Marcus, B. (2019) 'The next #metoo movement: older women confront ageism'. Available from: www.chicagotribune.com/opinion/commentary/ct-perspec-metoo-ageism-older-women-discrimination-0321-20190320-story.html

[15] You can listen to Ashton Applewhite's 2107 TED talk, 'Let's end ageism', here: www.ted.com/speakers/ashton_applewhite

[16] For example: Haynes, K. (2012) 'Body beautiful? Gender, identity and the body in professional services firms', *Gender, Work and Organizations*, 19 (5), 489–507.

Kenny, E. J., and Donnelly, R. (2019) 'Navigating the gender structure in information technology: how does this affect the experiences and behaviours of women?', *Human Relations*. DOI: 10.1177/0018726719828449

Trethewey, A. (2001) 'Reproducing and resisting the master narrative of decline: midlife professional women's experiences of aging', *Management Communication Quarterly*, 15 (2), 183–226.

[17] Beard, M. (2013) 'Mary Beard suffers "truly vile" online abuse after Question Time'. Available from: www.theguardian.com/media/2013/jan/21/mary-beard-suffers-twitter-abuse

[18] Hakim, C. (2010) 'Erotic capital', *European Sociological Review*, 26 (5), 499–518.

[19] Karpf, A. (2014) *How to age*. London: Pan Macmillan.

Chapter 3: The invisible force field of history

[1] Foxcroft, L. (2009) *Hot flushes, cold science: a history of the modern menopause*. London: Granta Books.

[2] Ehrenreich, B., and English, D. (2005) *For her own good: two centuries of expert's advice to women*. New York: Anchor Books.

Gatrell, C., Cooper, C. L., and Kossek, E. E. (2017) 'Maternal bodies as taboo at work: new perspectives on the marginalizing of senior-level women in organizations', *Academy of Management Perspectives*, 31 (3), 239–252.

[3] For example: Bullough, V. L. (1973) 'Medieval, medical and scientific views of women', *Viator*, 4, 485–501.

Maclean, I. (1980) *The Renaissance notion of woman: a study in the fortunes of scholasticism and medical science in European intellectual life.* Cambridge: Cambridge University Press.

[4] For example: Martin, E. (1992) *The woman in the body: a cultural analysis of reproduction.* Boston: Beacon Press.

Nettleton, S. (2006) *The sociology of health and illness* (2nd edition). Oxford: Blackwell.

[5] Schiebinger, L. (1987) 'Skeletons in the closet: the first illustrations of the female skeleton in eighteenth century anatomy', in Gallagher, C., and Laquer, T. (eds), *The making of the modern body: sexuality and society in the nineteenth century.* Berkeley: University of California Press, p. 47.

[6] Ibid., p. 43.

[7] Annandale, E. (2009) *Women's health and social change.* New York: Routledge.

Rosenberg, R. (1975) 'In search of woman's nature 1850–1920', *Feminist Studies*, 3, 141–150.

[8] Levine-Clark, M. (2004) *Beyond the reproductive body: the politics of women's health and work in early Victorian England.* Columbus: Ohio State University Press.

[9] Ehrenreich, B., and English, D. (2005) *For her own good: two centuries of expert's advice to women.* New York: Anchor Books, p. 526.

[10] Showalter, E. (1987) *The female malady: women, madness and English culture, 1930–1980.* New York: Penguin.

[11] See above, and Laquer, T. (1990) *Making sex: body and gender from the Greeks to Freud.* Cambridge: Harvard University Press.

[12] Dana, C. L. (1915) 'Suffrage a cult of self and sex', *New York Times* (online archive), 27 June.

[13] Russett, C. E. (1989) *Sexual science: the Victorian construction of womanhood.* Cambridge: Harvard University Press.

[14] Fine, C. (2010) *Delusions of gender: the real science behind sex differences.* London: Icon Books.

[15] Darwin, C. (1900) *The descent of man, and selection in relation to sex* (2nd edition). New York: P. F. Collier & Son.

[16] Roosevelt, T. (1908). Address to the First International Congress in America on the Welfare of the Child, under the auspices of the National Congress of Mothers. Washington, DC.

17 Sharp, I., and Stibb, M. (eds) (2017) *Women activists between war and peace: Europe, 1918–1923*. London: Bloomsbury.
18 Oakley, A. (1985) *The sociology of housework*. Oxford: Basil Blackwell.
19 Watkins, E. S. (2007) *The estrogen elixir: a history of hormone replacement therapy in America*. Baltimore: Johns Hopkins University Press.
20 Smith, M. C. (1991) *A social history of the minor tranquilizers: the quest for small comfort in the age of anxiety*. New York: Pharmaceuticals Product Press.
Speaker, S. L. (1997) 'From "happiness pills" to "national nightmare": changing cultural assessment of minor tranquilizers in America, 1955–1980', *Journal of the History of Medicine*, 52, 34.
Healey, D. (1997) *The antidepressant era*. Cambridge: Harvard University Press.
21 Rudman, L. A., and Glick, P. (2008) *The social psychology of gender: how power and intimacy shape gender relations*. London: The Guilford Press, p. 294.
22 Gatrell, C., Cooper, C. L., and Kossek, E. E. (2017) 'Maternal bodies as taboo at work: new perspectives on the marginalizing of senior-level women in organizations', *Academy of Management Perspectives*, 31 (3), 239–252.
23 As above, and: Prentice, D. A., and Carranza, E. (2002) 'What women and men should be, shouldn't be, are allowed to be and don't have to be: the contents of prescriptive gender stereotypes', *Psychology of Women Quarterly*, 26, 261–281.
Rudman, L. A., and Glick, P. (2001) 'Prescriptive gender stereotypes and backlash toward agentic women', *Journal of Social Issues*, 57, 732–762.
24 Rudman, L. A., and Glick, P. (2008) *The social psychology of gender: how power and intimacy shape gender relations*. London: The Guilford Press, p. 294.
25 Herndon, J. G. (2010) 'The grandmother effect: implications for studies on aging and cognition', *Gerontology*, 56 (1), 73–79.
26 For example: Eagly, A. H. (2007) 'Female leadership advantage and disadvantage: resolving the contradictions', *Psychology of Women Quarterly*, 31(1), 1–12.
Paustian-Underdahl, S. C., Walker, L. S., and Woehr, D. J. (2014) 'Gender and perceptions of leadership effectiveness: a meta-analysis of contextual moderators', *Journal of Applied Psychology*, 99 (6), 1129–1145.

Hoyt, C. L. (2010) 'Women, men, and leadership: exploring the gender gap at the top', *Social and Personality Psychology Compass*, 4 (7), 484–498.

[27] Sattari, N., et al. (2022) 'Dismantling "benevolent sexism"', *Harvard Business Review*, https://hbr.org/2022/06/dismantling-benevolent-sexism

[28] Baron-Cohen, S. (2003) *The essential difference: men, women and the extreme male brain*. London: Allen Lane.

[29] Pinker, S. (2008) *The sexual paradox: men, women, and the real gender gap*. New York: Scribner.

[30] Brizendine, L. (2007) *The female brain*. London: Bantam Press.

[31] See above references, including: Krivkovich, A., et al. (2022) 'Women in the Workplace'. Download report at: www.mckinsey.com/featured-insights/diversity-and-inclusion/women-in-the-workplace

House of Commons Library (2022) 'Women and the UK economy'. Download report at: https://commonslibrary.parliament.uk/research-briefings/sn06838/

Roffey Park (2022) 'Female leadership in the workplace'. Available from: www.roffeypark.ac.uk/knowledge-and-learning-resources-hub/female-lworkplace-building-a-workplace-culture-of-gender-balance-and-inclusivity/

Topping, A. (2022) 'Companies with female leaders outperform those dominated by men, data shows', www.theguardian.com, 6 March.

[32] Williams, Z. (2015) 'Feminazi: the go-to term for trolls out to silence women', *The Guardian*, 15 September.

Chapter 4: The fragile threshold of midlife

[1] Whyte, D. (2009) *The three marriages: reimagining work, self and relationship*. London: Penguin Books.

[2] Bridges, W. (2004) *Transitions: making sense of life's changes* (2nd edition). New York: De Capo Lifelong Books.

Bridges, W. (2017) *Managing transitions: making the most of change* (25th anniversary edition). New York: De Capo Lifelong Books.

[3] Mavin, S., and Grandy, G. (2016) 'A theory of abject appearance: women elite leaders' intra-gender "management" of bodies and appearance', *Human Relations*, 69 (5), 1095–1120.

[4] Hodges, J. (2012) 'The transition of midlife women from organisational into self-employment', *Gender in Management*, 27 (3), 186–201.

[5] Coverman, S. (1989) 'Role overload, role conflict and stress: addressing consequences of multiple role demands', *Social Forces*, 67 (4), 965–982.

[6] Hochschild, A. R. (1997) *The time bind: when work becomes home and home becomes work*. New York: Owl Books.

[7] Mills, E. (2022) www.noon.org.uk/meet-the-queenagers-executive-summary/

Chapter 5: Menopause: facts and frictions

[1] Brewis, J. (2022) 'The ball is now firmly in the government's court to break menopause taboos', www.peoplemanagement.co.uk, 6 September.

[2] Webber, A. (2023) 'Menopause protected characteristic idea rejected', www.personneltoday.com, 24 January.

[3] House of Commons Women and Equalities Commission (2022) 'Menopause and the workplace', www.parliament.uk.

Brewis, J., Beck, V., Davies, A., and Matheson, J. (2017) *The effects of menopause transitions on women's economic participation in the UK*. Research Report for Department for Education.

CIPD (2019) *The menopause at work: a practical guide for people managers*. Available from: www.cipd.co.uk (1 March 2019).

Hardy, C., Griffiths, A., and Hunter, M. S. (2018b) 'Menopause and work: an overview of UK guidance, *Occupational Medicine*, 68 (9), 580-586.

Griffiths, A., et al. (2006) 'Women police officers: ageing, work and health'. Report for the British Association of Women Police Officers.

National Union of Teachers (2014) 'Teachers working through the menopause, guidance for members in England and Wales'. December.

[4] Geddes, L. (2022) 'From vaginal laser treatment to spa breaks – it's the great menopause gold rush'. Available from: www.theguardian.com/lifeandstyle/2022/jan/26/from-vaginal-laser-treatment-to-spa-breaks-its-the-great-menopause-gold-rush

[5] WHO Scientific Group (1994) Research on the menopause in the 1990s. Geneva. Available from: www.who.int/iris/handle/10665/41841 (accessed April 2015).

Deeks, A. A., and McCabe, M. P. (2001) 'Menopausal stage and age and perceptions of body image', *Psychology and Health*, 16, 367–379.

Blake, J. (2006) 'Menopause: evidence based practice', *Best Practice and Research in Clinical Obstetrics and Gynaecology*, 20(6), 799–839.

[6] Geddes, 'From vaginal laser treatment'.

[7] Ibid.

[8] E.g. Hunter M., Gentry-Maharaj, A., Ryan, A., Burnell, M., Lanceley, A., Fraser, L., Jacobs, I., and Menon, U. (2012) 'Prevalence, frequency and problem rating of hot flushes persist in older postmenopausal women: impact of age, body mass index, hysterectomy, hormone therapy use, lifestyle and mood in a cross-sectional cohort study of 10,418 British women aged 54–65', *BJOG: An International Journal of Obstetrics and Gynaecology*, 119, 40–50.

[9] House of Commons Women and Equalities Commission, 'Menopause and the workplace', p. 7.

[10] Social Issues Research Centre – SIRC (2002) 'Jubilee women. Fiftysomething women – lifestyle and attitudes now and fifty years ago'.

[11] Hvas, L. (2001) 'Positive aspects of the menopause: a qualitative study', *Maturitas*, 39, 11–17.

[12] Hunter, M., and Rendall, M. (2007) 'Bio-psycho-socio-cultural perspectives on menopause', *Best Practice and Research in Clinical Obstetrics and Gynaecology*, 21 (2), 261–274.

[13] For an extensive list, see Brewis, J., Beck, V., Davies, A., and Matheson, J. (2017) *The effects of menopause transitions on women's economic participation in the UK*. Research Report for Department for Education, pp. 42–43.

[14] As above, and for example, Jack, G., Riach, K., Bariola, E., Pitts, M., Schapper, J., and Sarrel, P. (2016) 'Menopause in the workplace: what employers should be doing', *Maturitas*, 85 (3), 88–95.

Griffiths, A., et al. (2016) 'EMAS recommendations for conditions in the workplace for menopausal women' *Maturitas*, 85 (March), 79–81.

Chapter 6: Who cares?

[1] For example: O'Neil, D., and Bilimoria, D. (2005) 'Women's career development phases: idealism, endurance and reinvention', *Career Development International*, 10 (3), 168–189.

Pringle, J. K., and Dixon, K. M. (2003) 'Reincarnating life in the careers of women', *Career Development International*, 8 (6), 291–300.

[2] Labour Policy Forum (2015) Commission on Older Women. Available from: www.policyforum.labour.org.uk/uploads/editor/files/Commission_on_Older_Women_final_report_April_2015.pdf

Perrons, D. (2016) *Confronting inequality: findings from the LSE Commission on Gender, Inequality and Power*. LSE Knowledge Exchange, London.

Scales, J., and Scase, R. (2000) 'Fit and fifty? A report prepared for the Economic and Social Research Council'. Economic and Social Research Council, Colchester.

[3] Marks, N. F., Bumpass, L. L., and Heyjung, J. (2005) 'Family roles and well-being during the middle life course'. In Brim, O. G., Ryff, C. D., and Kessler, R. C. (eds), *How healthy are we? A national study of well-being at midlife*. Chicago: University of Chicago Press, pp. 514–550.

Government Office for Science (2016) 'Future of an ageing population'. Download report at: https://assets.publishing.service.gov.uk/government/uploads/system/uploads/attachment_data/file/816458/future-of-an-ageing-population.pdf

Office for National Statistics (2019) 'Milestones, journeying through adulthood'. Download report at: www.ons.gov.uk/people populationandcommunity/populationandmigration/population estimates/articles/milestonesjourneyingthroughadulthood/2019-12-17

Office for National Statistics (2021) 'Families and households in the UK'. Download report at: www.ons. gov.uk/peoplepopulation andcommunity/birthsdeathsandmarriages/families/bulletins/familiesandhouseholds/2021

[4] Fuller, J. B., and Raman, M. (2019) 'The caring company: how employers can help employees manage their caregiving responsibilities, while reducing costs and increasing productivity'. Harvard Business School Publishing.

[5] BMJ (2012) 'The health and development of children born to older mothers in the United Kingdom: observational study using longitudinal cohort data'. Available from: https://doi.org/10.1136/bmj.e5116

[6] Office for National Statistics (2017) *Childbearing for women born in different years: England and Wales, 2017*. London.

[7] MIDUS study: Brim, O. G., Ryff, C. D., and Kessler, R. C. (2005) 'Studies on successful midlife development'. In Brim, O. G., Ryff, C. D., and Kessler, R. C. (eds), *How healthy are we? A national study of well-being at midlife*. Chicago: University of Chicago Press, pp. 1–34.

[8] Office for National Statistics (2017) *Childbearing for women born in different years*.

[9] Ibid.

[10] Khazan, O. (2018) 'The rise of older mothers', www.theatlantic.com. Available from: www.theatlantic.com/health/archive/2018/05/the-rise-of-older-mothers/560555/

[11] Jarvie, R., Letherby, G., and Stenhouse, E. (2015) 'Renewed older motherhood/mothering: a qualitative exploration', *Journal of Women & Aging*. DOI: 10.1080/08952841.2014.927728

[12] Smajdor, A. (2009) 'Between fecklessness and selfishness: is there a biologically optimal time for motherhood?' In Simonstein F. (ed.), *Reprogen-ethics and the future of gender*. International Library of Ethics, Law, and the New Medicine, vol. 43. Dordrecht: Springer, pp. 105–117.

[13] Roberts, Y. (2015) 'The agony and ecstasy of becoming an older mother', *The Observer*, 30 August.

[14] Power, K. (2020) 'The COVID-19 pandemic has increased the care burden of women and families', *Sustainability, Science, Practice & Policy*, 16 (1).

[15] World Health Organization (2021) 'Adolescent mental health'. Available from: www.who.int/news-room/fact-sheets/detail/adolescent-mental-health

[16] Office for National Statistics (2022) 'Differences in time use after coronavirus restrictions were lifted'. Available from: www.ons.gov.uk/peoplepopulationandcommunity/healthandsocialcare/healthandwellbeing/datasets/differencesintimeuseaftercoronavirusrestrictionswerelifteddukmarch2022

[17] Women's Budget Group (2022) *Creating a caring economy: a call to action*. Available from: https://wbg.org.uk/wp-content/uploads/2020/10/WBG-Report-v10.pdf

[18] ONS (Census, 2021) 'Household satellite accounts, UK 2015 and 2106'. Available from: www.ons.gov.uk/economy/nationalaccounts/satelliteaccounts/articles/householdsatelliteaccounts/2015and2016estimates

[19] Slaughter, A. M. (2012) 'Why women still can't have it all', *The Atlantic Magazine*. Available from: www.theatlantic.com/magazine/archive/2012/07/why-women-still-cant-have-it-all/309020

Chapter 7: Facing mortality

[1] Kets de Vries, M. F. R. (2014) *Death and the executive: encounters with the "Stealth" Motivator*. INSEAD: Faculty and Research Working Paper. Downloaded at: http://ssrn.com/abstract=2388216.

[2] Kets de Vries, M. F. R. (1994) 'Can you manage the rest of your life?', *European Management Journal*, 12 (2), 133–137.

Kets de Vries, M. F. R. (1995) *Life and death in the executive fast lane: essays on irrational organizations and their leaders*. San Francisco: Jossey-Bass.

[3] Kets de Vries, M. F. R. (1978) 'The midcareer conundrum', *Organizational Dynamics*, 7 (2), 42–62.

[4] Kets de Vries, *Death and the executive*, p. 2.

[5] Becker, E. (1973, reprinted 2018) *The denial of death*. Souvenir Press. Hollis, J. (2006) *Finding meaning in the second half of life*. New York: Gotham Books.

[6] Kets de Vries, *Death and the executive*, p. 4.

[7] Hollis, J. (1993) *The middle passage: from misery to meaning in midlife*. Toronto: Inner City Books.

[8] Evans, M. (2017) *The persistence of gender inequality*. Cambridge: Polity Press.

Chapter 8: Motivation and midlife

[1] Kristeva, J., and Oliver, K. (ed.) (2002) *The portable Kristeva*. New York: Columbia University Press.

[2] Ibid., p. 39, pp. 12, 502.

[3] Contemporary workplaces are still surprisingly influenced by old lifespan assumptions, including: Erikson, E. H. (1959) *Identity and the life cycle*. New York: W. W. Norton; and Levinson, D. (1979) *The seasons of a man's life*. New York: Ballantine.

[4] Karp, D. A. (1987) 'Professionals beyond midlife: some observations on work satisfaction in the fifty to sixty year old decade', *Journal of Aging Studies*, 1 (3), 209–223.

[5] Tupper, H., and Ellis, S. (2020) *The squiggly career – ditch the ladder, discover opportunity, design your career*. London: Portfolio Penguin.

[6] Gordon, J. R., Beatty, J. E., and Whelan, K. S. (2002) 'The midlife transition of professional women with children', *Women in Management Review*, 17 (7), 328–341.

[7] Gersick, C. J. C., and Kram, K. E. (2002) 'High achieving women at midlife', *Journal of Management Inquiry*, 11 (2), 104–127.

[8] For example: Gibbs, N. (2005) 'Midlife crisis? Bring it on!', *Time Magazine*, 63, 52–66. Muhlbauer, V. and Chrisler, J. C. (2012) 'Women, power, and aging: an introduction', *Women & Therapy*, 35, 137–144.

[9] Vaillant, G. E. (2012) *Aging well*. Boston: Little Brown & Co.

[10] Gullette, M. M. (2004) *Aged by culture*. Chicago: University of Chicago Press, p. 17.

[11] Bridges, W. (2017) *Managing transitions: making the most of change (25th anniversary edition)*. New York: De Capo Lifelong Books.

[12] Kristeva and Oliver, *The portable Kristeva*, p. 502.

Chapter 9: The sparkle of female genius!

[1] Kristeva, J., and Oliver, K. (ed.) (2002) *The portable Kristeva*. New York: Columbia University Press, p. 403.

[2] Mead, M. (1959) 'Student and teacher of human ways: anthropologist Margaret Mead, America's best–known woman scientist, gives modern America some tips for improvement'. Available from: www.originallifemagazines.com/product/life-magazine-september-14-1959

[3] For example, here are two of the four studies: Chopik, W. J., Bel, E. S., and Smith, J. (2015) 'Changes in optimism are associated with changes in health over time among older adults', *Social Psychology Personal Science*, 6 (7).
Blanchflower, D. G., and Oswald, A. J. (2008) 'Is well-being U-shaped over the lifecycle?', *Social Science & Medicine*, 66, 1733–1749.

[4] Hakim, C. (2010) 'Erotic capital', *European Sociological Review*, 26 (5), 499–518.

[5] Isopahkala-Bouret, U. (2017) '"It's a great benefit to have gray hair!": the intersection of gender, aging, and visibility in midlife professional women's narratives', *Journal of Women and Aging*, 29 (3), 267–277.

[6] Sarkar, M., & Fletcher, D. (2014) 'Ordinary magic, extraordinary performance: psychological resilience and thriving in high achievers', *Sport, Exercise, and Performance Psychology, 3*(1), 46–60.
Reivich, K., and Shatté, A. (2002) *The resilience factor: 7 essential skills for overcoming life's inevitable obstacles*. New York: Broadway Books.

[7] Tedeschi, G. (2020) *Growth after trauma*. Available from: https://hbr.org/2020/07/growth-after-trauma
Jayawickreme, E., Infurna, F. J., Alajak, K., Blackie, L. E., Chopik, W. J., Chung, J. M., ... and Zonneveld, R. (2021) 'Post-traumatic growth as positive personality change: challenges, opportunities, and recommendations', *Journal of Personality*, 89 (1), 145-165.

[8] Eleanor Mills, Founder & Editor in Chief. www.noon.org.uk/meet-the-queenagers-executive-summary/

Chapter 10: Rewriting the rules of career success

[1] The situation is well summarized in this news report: Peachey, K. (2022) 'Pensions scandal, thousands more women underpaid'. Available from: www.bbc.co.uk/news/business-62085429

[2] Sinclair, A. (2007) *Leadership for the disillusioned: moving beyond myths and heroes to leadership that liberates*. Sydney: Allen & Unwin.

[3] Appignanesi, L. (2009) *Mad, bad and sad*. London: Virago Books.

[4] Terjesen, S. (2005) 'Senior women managers' transition to entrepreneurship, leveraging embedded career capital', *Career Development International*, 10 (3), 246–259.

Hodges, J. (2012) 'The transition of midlife women from organisational into self-employment', *Gender in Management*, 27 (3), 186–201.

[5] Rose, A. (2019) The Alison Rose review of female entrepreneurship. Available from: www.gov.uk/government/publications/the-alison-rose-review-of-female-entrepreneurship

[6] Irvine, S., et al. (2022) *Women and UK economy*. House of Commons Library.

[7] Silverman, R. (2018) *The age advantage: how female 'olderpreneurs' are starting businesses in midlife*. www.thetelegraph.co.uk

[8] The story of Cherry Harker, ibid.

[9] Moore, I. (2017) 'Older female entrepreneurs'. Download report at: https://olderwomeninbusiness.com/wp-content/uploads/2017/06/Older-Female-Entrepreneurship-Report-V5-041017-NG.pdf

Conclusion: A positive agenda for change

[1] Krivkovich, A., et al. (2022) 'Women in the workplace'. Download report at: www.mckinsey.com/featured-insights/diversity-and-inclusion/women-in-the-workplace

[2] Ibid., p. 5.

[3] Smith, M. (2022) 'It's a disastrous situation, women leaders are leaving companies at the highest rate ever'. Available from: www.cnbc.com/2022/10/18/women-leaders-are-leaving-companies-at-highest-rate-ever-leanin-mckinsey-co-report.html

[4] Krivkovich et al., 'Women in the workplace', p. 7.

[5] Vinnicombe, S., and Tessaro, M. (2022) 'The Female FTSE Report, What works?', Cranfield School of Management. Download report at: www.cranfield.ac.uk/femaleftseboardreport

[6] Konrad, A., and Erkust, S. (2008) 'Critical mass. The impact of three or more women on corporate boards', *Organizational Dynamics*, 37 (2), 145–164.

[7] Eleanor Mills, Founder. www.noon.org.uk/meet-the-queenagers-executive-summary/

[8] Allende, I. (2007) View her TED talk at: www.ted.com/talks/isabel_allende_tales_of_passion?language=en

ABOUT THE AUTHOR

Dr Lucy Ryan has a well-earned reputation as a wise, vibrant leadership coach and a voice that leaders take seriously. With a master's in Positive Psychology and a PhD in Leadership, she has developed over 10,000 global leaders, blending psychology with practical, accessible guidance, encapsulated in her 2021 book, *Lunchtime Learning for Leaders*. Throughout her career she has been a passionate advocate for the retention and promotion of women and in this book she draws on her PhD research and extensive experience of working with female leaders to challenge assumptions of women over 50 in the workplace and promote their strengths. Lucy is a senior lecturer at the University of East London and a visiting research fellow at the University of Liverpool.

ACKNOWLEDGEMENTS

This book has been some years in the making and there is at least a chapter of thanks for those who made it possible, but brevity in this case is better!

I am indebted to the patient supervision of Professor Caroline Gatrell through the four years of my PhD, and the reason this book exists. Caroline took me on as a student when others turned their heads away from the subject matter, and her patient, guiding hand was exactly what I needed. She remains a steadfast advocate for the academic visibility of older women. Professor Sue Vinnicombe CBE was my examiner and I will be forever grateful to her for her research in this field and for enabling the viva to be a positive space – often a rarity in the academic world.

I have a very big thank you to make to the many inspiring – and exceptionally busy – female managers and leaders who gave me time to interview them about how they experienced their professional lives at middle age. Their wisdom about the workplace, their generosity of insight and willingness to share candid stories about their lives transformed the nature of my study. Each day of research became a joyful, unexpected learning experience.

Turning an academic piece of work into a business book requires the professional eye and guidance of a good publisher, and Alison Jones, Director of Practical Inspiration Publishing, is, in my humble view, the best. She advises, challenges, and encourages you to keep going, to try again, and to never forget the reader! She is a tour de force of motivation. Alison Gray is exactly the kind of editor any would-be author could wish for. She has a keen eye for detail, yet never loses sight of the big picture. Her brilliant direction is delivered with warmth, heart, and an understanding that writing can be a vulnerable process! My appreciation extends to the whole team at Practical Inspiration Publishing, who manage to make you feel a special part of the publishing family.

I am grateful to my tribe of 'revolting women' many of whom have trod the journey path of this book from early days of research to publication, as well as taking time to read the manuscript and provide me with reassurance! They are, simply, wonderful human beings. My sincere love and thanks to Diane Herbert, Lise Lewis, Susie Cleverly, Claire Schimmer, Alison Sedgwick Taylor, Janie van Hool, Fiona Parashar, Jo Hale, Rachel Dymond, and Jax Brabazon.

Most of all, I'm grateful to my family. My mum, Elizabeth, remains interested in every project I tackle, albeit with a raised eyebrow! My sister, Sarah, remains one of only (probably) four people to read my PhD (she still insists she has a vicarious PhD), and my kids, Ames and Livvy, are my 'chief encouragers' who make me feel very proud. But Steve, my partner of 35 years, is my steadfast ally. He offers love, laughter, and tea in equal measure. He's always there to pick me up and set me back on my feet again. And he's stopped asking me if this is my last book!

INDEX